# THE SERIOUS
# JOB SEEKER

*By Cici Mattiuzzi*

Printed in the United States of America

*Design by Loren Crosier*

Library of Congress Control Number: 2015904974
CreateSpace Independent Publishing Platform, North Charleston, SC

First Printing, March 2015

ISBN-13: 978-1508766094
ISBN-10: 1508766096

www.seriousjobseeker.com

# ACKNOWLEDGMENTS

I am so blessed to be able to help people define who they are and find their purpose in life.

This book would not be possible without the inspiration from countless job seekers who have sought my help.

The questions asked and dilemmas faced inspired me to write.

I am grateful for the help and support of my husband Paul throughout this project.

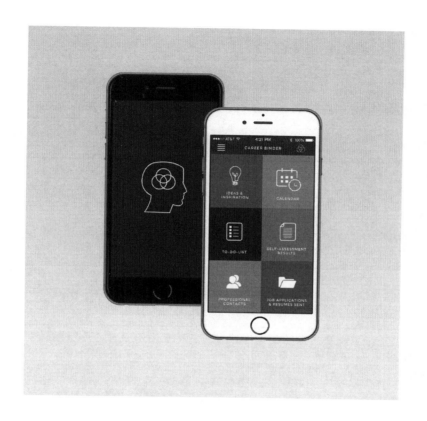

## GET THE SERIOUS JOB SEEKER APP

Take skill assessment tests and keep up with your *career binder* on your mobile device.  *Includes:* assessments and exercises, notes, professional contacts, task-manager, calendar, and more!

*Available in the Google Play store and iTunes May 2015!*

www.seriousjobseeker.com

TABLE OF CONTENTS

# SELF-ASSESSMENT

# MORE SELF-ASSESSMENT

# PUTTING IT ALL TOGETHER

# JOB SEARCH STRATEGY

# RESUMES AND PORTFOLIOS

# INTERVIEWS

## SALARY NEGOTIATIONS

## REFERENCES

# WHICH OFFER SHOULD YOU TAKE?

# SURVIVING A LAYOFF

# MANAGING YOUR CAREER

INTRODUCTION

*The Serious Job Seeker* is a practical guide to career choice, change, search and success. To be a serious job seeker is to develop a planful life. This book will help you to develop a career-life plan that allows you to thrive.

The lessons in this book are for anyone engaged at any level in the process of choosing a career, finding a job, making a change, or moving up the ladder.

If you do the work - this book will guide you to your perfect career!

You will learn all of the critical 5 elements of a solid career plan: *Job Search Organization, Market Awareness, Career Focus, Self-Assessment, Professional Presentation, and Job Search Strategy.*

*The Serious Job Seeker* will guide you along step-by-step through all of these challenges and help you to make the most of your own personal career adventure.

- Creating a job search binder
- Understanding the impact of market forces
- Identifying your core strengths - your motivated skills, interests, goals, and values
- Researching your career options
- Creating spot-on resumes and cover letters
- Identifying and targeting companies that let you be your best self
- Developing a solid strategy to get the job you really want

Doing a self-assessment and conducting thorough career research will be critical to your self-presentation and your effectiveness in securing the position you want.

You will need to be prepared to tell an employer that you have the skills *they* are looking for, where you have used them before, and that you are motivated to perform.

After you convince an employer you are the best candidate for the job, you will need to convince them that you are well worth the salary you are going to negotiate.

You are also going to learn that career awareness and focus will remain relevant throughout the course of your work life. There should never be a time when you are not prepared to take advantage of opportunity or to seek the path of your choice.

# CAREER PLANNING CHALLENGES:

*The Tasks that Lie Ahead...*

## 1.0

# CAREER PLANNING CHALLENGES

As a serious job seeker, you will face a series of challenges or tasks to be mastered. There are actually a number of ways you might go about finding a job, but you want to do it the smart way and in the most effective fashion, especially if you want great results.

You can think of it like taking a vacation in a place you have never visited before. You could just grab a bag and go, but it makes more sense to do some planning, read about the locale, talk to people who have been there, make a packing list, and get some reservations. There are many ways to ruin a vacation. Most of the pitfalls can be anticipated and avoided.

*In planning your career, there are five challenges you face:*

Organization

Awareness

Focus

Strategy

Presentation

What I have found is that when students or clients decide to see me for individual career assistance, they are invariably focused on or stuck on one of these specific challenges.

## ORGANIZATION

*Organization* refers to your ability to maintain documents, notes, contacts, correspondence, schedules and appointments in an orderly fashion. The serious job seeker knows that career planning involves developing a significant level of organization around the career planning and job search process.

For your job search, it is absolutely essential that you put together a binder to keep track of the ideas you develop, the contacts you make, the correspondence you have sent, the information you obtain, the applications you have filed, the companies you have researched, the tasks you need to complete, and so on. Your career binder is where you will keep your "daily to do" list. Knowing what you need to do tomorrow is important, because if you waste your time, you waste your life ...

## AWARENESS

*Awareness* refers to your understanding of events happening in the world around you.

Every day in the news, there are reports about social, political, economic, demographic and technological changes that will impact the labor market and alter the range of occupational choices. Often times, things will change in what seems like a heartbeat. Other trends are slow moving and long lasting.

Your challenge is to pay attention to the news and to think about how different events might ripple out in some way that changes the dynamics of the job market. Will an opportunity be created? Or will an industry die? What doors will open and which ones might slam shut?

Perhaps you have heard of "the butterfly effect." It's the idea that the flapping of a butterfly's wings will change the atmosphere ever so slightly, and that this seemingly insignificant change could ultimately result in a tornado blowing across some other part of the world. That is what you are looking for as you maintain awareness.

## FOCUS

**Focus** refers to the task of gathering information about yourself. In other words: self-assessment.

You need to make certain that you understand what you really want to do. Serious job seekers do not start out expecting that they will simply settle on what they thought they were supposed to do or what they think they are qualified for.

What you are looking for is the position that will provide you with career satisfaction. Satisfying work empowers you and plays a critical role in psychological health and well being.

Satisfaction depends partly on performing tasks that you enjoy. It involves using the skills and the knowledge that you enjoy using and that you are motivated to use. When you do what you like or what interests you, you are more likely to be successful, and that leads to greater satisfaction.

Satisfaction at work also comes from employment that is consistent with your needs, values and priorities. Different things are important to different people, and at different career stages. Your career should satisfy both your short term and long term goals.

Somewhere out there, there is a ideal position for you. But it is not just a matter of skills and interests. You also have to consider where you want to be located and what type of lifestyle you wish to pursue. You need to know what type of people you would enjoy working with, and what type of people and working conditions you might find intolerable.

## STRATEGY

**Strategy** refers to your ability to conduct the career development and job search process with a plan, and in a proactive and systematic fashion.

*What you will learn is that the fundamental strategy for finding a job involves the simple act of gathering career information.*

You have probably heard it said a thousand times that most job openings are never posted or advertised. You've heard it said that people find jobs primarily through their contacts. This is essentially true, and this insight is the key to your job search strategy.

It is not the case, however, that you can count on finding a job just because you know people, or because you have good luck. What it means is that you need to get to know people, and to learn what they know, and to organize your luck.

You will need to talk to people about what they do, and to ask them for the names of other people you can speak to. It is much easier to speak with someone about what they do, rather than why they should hire you. And every time you speak with someone and ask them whom else you might speak with, you will be amplifying your list of contacts. You will also be gaining invaluable information about what you really want to do and about those who are most likely to hire you.

The more people you speak with, the more likely it is that you will find that perfect situation. The more contacts you make, the better the chances are that someone in a position to make a hiring decision will make the decision to hire you. The basic strategy involves getting to know all that you can, and getting yourself known to the people who can make it happen for you.

This does not mean that you will ignore employment advertisements or jobs that are posted online. You may get lucky and find a position that is listed somewhere, a job that is perfect for you and for which you are exactly the right candidate. But simply looking at the want ads, submitting applications and hoping that lightning will strike is not the way that the serious job seeker goes about the task.

The serious job seeker will in fact look at the want ads and submit applications, but will always keep in mind that this is not enough.

To make the strategy work, you need to learn how to organize your time, how to find information in publications, how to find "what's out there," how to make contacts, and how to approach informational interviews. The checklist of daily and weekly activities that you need to follow is quite specific and reads like a job description itself. You will also need to avoid any of the "costly errors that kill job offers."

## PRESENTATION

*Presentation* refers to your ability to look your best in person, on paper and on the phone.

Presentation is about what you put on your resume and how you organize and format it. It's also about interview skills: knowing how to prepare, knowing what questions to ask and knowing what questions you need to be ready to answer. Presentation is about thank you letters and letters of reference, and in the end, it's about salary negotiation strategies.

When you start working on your presentation, you will understand why all of the self-assessment exercises were important. If you skip over the self-assessment, you are not going to be able to put your best foot forward on your resume or application. You won't be prepared to describe your skills in a way that will make an employer take notice. You won't be prepared to explain why you are a good fit for the job, why you are motivated to perform and how you can contribute. In an interview, a potential employer will probably ask questions that have little to do with the job and a lot to do with getting to know you as a person. You need to be prepared to present yourself in a favorable light, and you can't do that if you haven't gone through the process of sorting out who you really are. And when it comes down to that last and final step of negotiating a salary, you have to be able to present a good argument as to why you are worth the extra money you are going to be asking for.

## THE CAREER PLANNING CHALLENGE IN THUMBNAIL FORM:

- You will need to gather a fair amount of information and keep it organized at every stage in the process.

- You will need to research the world-of-work and develop an awareness of what's going on in that world.

- You need to focus on knowing who you are by conducting a careful self-assessment of your skills and interests.

- You will need to develop and implement an effective job search strategy, do it correctly and avoid mistakes.

- You need to look good in person, on the phone and on paper.

# 02

# GETTING ORGANIZED

*Your Career Binder should be constructed with dividers. It needs to be divided into five sections, labeled as follows:*

| | |
|---|---|
| 01. | Ideas and Inspiration |
| 02. | Timelines/Calendar/To Do Lists |
| 03. | Career Plan/Job Search Strategy |
| 04. | Contacts |
| 05. | Job Applications/Resumes Sent |

## 2.0

## GETTING ORGANIZED WITH YOUR CAREER BINDER, ABSOLUTELY ESSENTIAL!

*If you are serious about finding a good job, the right job, you need to gather information and keep it organized.* You need to be able to access the information you need when you need it, quickly and efficiently. Don't assume that it's OK to just create another stack of papers on your desk or that you can just throw everything into one drawer. This is serious business.

The *BEST* way to organize your job search is to put together a binder to keep track of the ideas, applications, and contacts you make during your job search. In fact, *to keep your career search materials organized, a Career Binder is absolutely essential!*

A career binder is particularly helpful when you are working with a career coach. Don't even think about coming to see me in my office if you don't have a career binder! I'll talk to you even if you just have some papers in hand, showing that you have given some thought to your career search. But if you want me to pay serious attention, I'm going to want to see your career binder.

For the last two sections (Contacts and Job Applications/Resumes Sent), you need to have a set of A to Z index dividers.

*Don't make the mistake of trying to file everything online or on your computer or on your cell phone!* This is hands-on stuff and there is a lot of information you need to have in hard copy where you can touch it and take notes (you can worry about saving trees after you get a job).

For many of the tasks involved in finding a job, you are going to have to keep pen and paper handy, and to get in the habit of hitting the print button.

*Make sure you read each of the five sections that follow and to look at the templates to be used for organizing.*

### YOUR CAREER BINDER: THE IDEAS & INSPIRATION SECTION

*The Ideas and Inspirations section should include some blank paper so that when you have an idea, no matter how silly it may seem, you can jot it down.* You will also want to insert articles you print from the web or clip from the newspapers, professional journals and magazines about people and companies doing interesting or innovative things, ideas that you may want to follow up on later.

*Sometimes, the most ridiculous idea can turn out to be the perfect career.*

Your idea may involve a new invention, a needed service, or a business opportunity just waiting to be exploited.

An inspiration might come from a story about an industry that is either flourishing or floundering. From either the good news or the bad, you might recognize a niche to be filled where your talents and skills are a perfect fit.

If you are open to ideas, you may realize that there are organizations that hire people just like you, or people with your interests, even though the industry seems far afield from what you have studied or set your sights on.

Most of the ideas and inspirations that come to you will be of little or no value. But you never know when lightning will strike.

In 1977, the founder of Digital Equipment Corporation (DEC) was quoted saying: "There is no reason anyone would want a computer in their home." Steve Jobs and Steve Wozniak had a different idea. They thought if they wanted their own computer, so did everyone else. Later, Jobs also figured out that everyone needed a computer in their pocket.

Larry Page and Sergey Brin were students at Stanford when they were inspired by the idea that the world wide web needed to be searched. A simple idea, with no apparent monetary value was launched with a silly name that would soon become a verb (you can google that).

One of my students was fascinated with explosives. His career inspiration came when he learned that airbags are powered by explosive charges and that there must be a job for him in the auto industry.

Ideas and inspiration are like fish swimming by. If you fail to catch them when you see them, they just disappear. Even if it seems like a long shot, write it down! ... or clip it out of the paper.

## STAYING ORGANIZED WITH A SUCCESS TIMELINE

Getting organized requires that you create a *Success Timeline*, maintain a *Calendar* and keep a *Daily To Do List*.

**These are your control devices.** They allow you to organize your time so that you can get done what you need to do to achieve your goals. There are plenty of time robbers in everyone's life. Most people feel that someone else controls their time. Demanding professors, spouses, parents, friends, and children, to name a few, control your life. Many job seekers find that they fritter away their time and then wonder why they have not yet gotten a job.

The reality is that it takes between 3 and 6 months to get a job in just about any labor market- good or bad. If you are not doing the right things or if you are disorganized you will be sabotaging your efforts.

Your *Success Timeline* is the larger view of what you plan to accomplish and when. There are a lot of steps involved in finding a great job, and as you progress through the tasks and assignments in this book, your activity Timeline will develop and change. It will become more focused and detailed as you learn more about what you need to do.

Fasten your seat belt. There are a lot of things you will be doing as we progress!

*Let's take a look at a sample Success Timeline on the next page.* This template is a starting point for developing your own Success Timeline. As your career search progresses, you will want to come back and modify your timeline so that you can keep focused on the big picture, beyond your daily to do list. *It will be especially important to come back and edit your Success Timeline after you finish the Goal Setting section of the self-assessment process.*

# SUCCESS TIMELINE

**01** *Week 1:*
Set up a Career Binder to organize the process

**02** *Weeks 1, 2 & 3:*
Read *serious job seeker* chapters 1 through 6 ...
complete the self-assessment exercises.

**03** *Weeks 3 & 4:*
Begin researching occupational areas of interest

Identify industries where interests fit

Research possible companies

Create list of good fit companies

Identify list of contacts

Network with family/friends/contacts

Cold call where you have no contacts

Develop and refine resume

**04** *Weeks 4 & 5:*
Practice interviewing w/friend

Research company before interview

Analyze job description before interview

**05** *Week 5 through rest of search :*
Do info interviewing (6 per week)

Send resume when appropriate

Revise resume for each company

**06** *3 months:*
Hopefully have a great job! If not, double down
and spend more time on your efforts or talk
to an expert who can assess your situation and
move you forward.

**07** *4th, 5th & 6th months:*
Continue info interviewing until you have job.

## STAYING ORGANIZED WITH A DAILY TO-DO LIST & CALENDAR

Every day, you need to map out your next day's activities by creating a Daily To Do List. That way nothing gets lost in the cracks.

*The four sections you need to fill in each day for your career search:*

> **Tasks to be Done**
> **Calls to be Made**
> **Appointments to be made**
> **Projects to work on**

*You can keep your To Do List updated online, but if you do, you need to print it out on a regular basis.* This is hands-on stuff, and you need to have it in hard copy where you can touch it, feel it and take notes. The other reason you want to keep a printed copy in your Career Binder is so that you can see how you are progressing with your daily tasks. You also want to make sure you have a record of everything you've accomplished.

## HERE IS A TO DO LIST TEMPLATE TO USE ... OR CREATE YOUR OWN. (P.27) ▶

*The Daily To Do List is meant to be immediate. It is meant to tell you exactly what you need to get done today. In reality ... you will also be using it to keep track of tasks that may take a few days or that may have a future deadline. There are some tasks that* you will want to schedule for upcoming days and that you will want to put on your Calendar. On Tuesday, you should be thinking ahead to what you will need to be doing on Thursday. Once you get in the habit of using a To Do List, it shouldn't take you long to figure out how to make it work for keeping track of tasks, and how to coordinate it with your calendar.

*Your Calendar is separate from your To Do List and is essential for keeping track of your scheduled appointments.*

You will be scheduling your time a couple of weeks in advance so that you can meet with the people you need to meet with to make things happen. You are going to be meeting busy people and you don't want to screw up by missing an appointment or scheduling two events at the same time.

You are becoming a busy person with a schedule that needs to be developed, maintained and adjusted on a constant basis. It is really easy to find a calendar template that you can print out. There's probably a calendar app on your computer already.

For the calendar, it's ok to go completely electronic or to buy an appointment book at the stationery store. However you do it, make sure it is handy and always with you and available. Whether you keep your Calendar in your Career Binder or you keep it separate, make sure that it's always with you.

So start planning and start looking at your Calendar and To Do Lists everyday ...

## YOUR CAREER BINDER: THE JOB SEARCH CONTACT NOTES SECTION

This section is for maintaining information about all the valuable contacts you will make. For each contact, you want to keep a business card and a page of notes.

Keeping track of your contacts seems like something you really should be doing just on your computer, where the search function can readily be accessed. But the reality is that you are not going to have essential information available when you need it if you don't have it on paper and on your computer. You don't want to lose track. You also need to be able to organize the business cards people will be giving you.

For the cards in your Career Binder, you want to buy of set of business card sheet protectors from any stationary store. Just slip a few into your binder and as you receive cards from people, keep them here for easy access.

You also need a Contact Form for more detailed record keeping. You are going to learn a lot about your field of interest and you don't want to let anything that is important get away from you. Taking notes is essential to staying on top of things in your job search, and it is a task that won't wait until you are back at your desk or you open up your laptop. Remember, this is your job ... getting the right job.

MANAGE YOUR "TO DO" LIST IN
*THE SERIOUS JOB SEEKER APP*
*SERIOUSJOBSEEKER.COM*

HERE IS A CONTACT FORM TEMPLATE (P.28) ▶ ... use it as is or as a starting point to develop your own. This one will give some ideas about the types of information you want to record for each person you meet or call.

## YOUR CAREER BINDER: THE JOB APPLICATIONS & RESUMES SENT SECTION

This is where you will store the documents that you send to companies that you apply with: position descriptions, copies of completed applications, cover letters, resumes - anything you sent.

The best way to organize your documents is to use "a to z" index dividers so you can keep your materials in alphabetical order by the company name.

If the employer calls in response to your application, you want to make sure that you're on the same page. You need these materials in hard copy because you will probably be sending slightly different versions of your documents for each job that you apply for. If a potential employer is asking you questions about your resume or application, you want to make certain you know what you said ... at the very least, you want to make certain that you know exactly what you put down on your resume for your "career objective."

And if the employer calls to screen you by phone, or if you need to prepare for an interview, you really want to be able to quickly find the job description. If an employer calls, nothing is less impressive than a candidate who cannot remember which job they applied for.

"Could you tell me which job we are talking about?" is a non-starter ...

# DAILY TO-DO LIST

*TASKS TO BE DONE:*

| | TASKS | NOTES |
|---|---|---|
| 1 | | |
| 2 | | |
| 3 | | |
| 4 | | |

*CALLS TO MAKE:*

| DATE/TIME | NAME | PHONE # | NOTES |
|---|---|---|---|
| | | | |
| | | | |
| | | | |
| | | | |
| | | | |

*APPOINTMENTS TO BE MADE:*

| DATE/TIME | APT. WITH | WHERE | NOTES |
|---|---|---|---|
| | | | |
| | | | |

*PROJECTS TO BE DONE:*

| | PROJECT | DUE DATE | NOTES |
|---|---|---|---|
| 1 | | | |
| 2 | | | |

# CONTACT FORM TEMPLATE

| | |
|---|---|
| **CONTACT DATE** | |
| **NAME** | |
| **TITLE OR POSITION** | |
| **COMPANY** | |
| **ADDRESS** | |
| **PHONE #** | |
| **CELL #** | |
| **EMAIL** | |
| **WEB ADDRESS** | |
| **NOTES** | • Take note of how you made this contact.<br>• Date each note and include follow-up steps and actions required.<br>• Document each contact with this person. |

ONLINE VERSION
*SERIOUSJOBSEEKER.COM*

# 03

# AWARENESS

## 3.0

# YOU NEED TO KNOW WHO'S HIRING!

Every day, things are happening in the economy and the world around you, things that might impact your career plans and your job aspirations.

Events across the street, across the country or across the world might impact your employment situation or the demand for your skills. At any given time there are job categories that are declining and others that are disappearing altogether. Economic disruptions, technology developments, political instability, fluctuations in the price of oil can all cause shifts that impact demand for labor.

***Your best insurance policy against unemployment is to keep yourself well informed.*** Knowing when to make a move is essential to your success ... not just today, or tomorrow, but for the rest of your career life. If you are a serious job seeker, your job is to know what industries are growing and what organizations are likely to be hiring.

And once you get a job, you will want to be aware of things that can disrupt your employment, before it becomes a crisis. When things change, the first ones to move are the lucky ones. It is like being on the Titanic when a company or industry is going down. If you are not one of the first ones off and into a lifeboat, you are going to be sucked down with everyone else. This isn't brain surgery.

Every day in the news, there are reports about social, political, economic, and technological changes that will impact the labor market and alter the range of occupational choices. Often times, things will change in what seems like a heartbeat. Other trends are slow moving and long lasting.

The outsourcing of jobs is a long term trend that has caused a significant decline in certain manufacturing jobs here in the US. The run up in health care costs over the past twenty years is also a long term trend.

In contrast, the 2007 meltdown in the mortgage lending industry happened almost overnight, and it created layoffs in areas as diverse as financial services and housing construction. The resulting shock to the stock market, the impact on interest rates and the tightening of credit sent ripples throughout the entire economy. In 2008, it became clear that it wasn't just a ripple, it was a recession. By early 2009, it became clear that the economy had gone into crisis mode. The resulting recession lasted for several years and continues to be felt in many industries.

Earlier, I mentioned "the butterfly effect." It's the idea that the flapping of a butterfly's wings will change the atmosphere ever so slightly, and that this seemingly insignificant change could ultimately result in a tornado blowing across some other part of the world. That is what you are looking for as you maintain awareness.

There are a lot of stories in the news reflecting ordinary and routine events. But many events that hardly seem newsworthy at all have implications that go far beyond what might immediately seem apparent. Think of it like dropping a pebble into a pond. One small stone sends ripples to the pond's farthest edges.

## 3.1

# CHANGE HAPPENS!

*Economic realities have changed in the past few decades. Lifetime job security no longer exists. Many if not most workers can expect to change jobs every three to five years and to make major career shifts three to five times in their lifetimes.*

Workers across the globe are having to reinvent themselves regularly to maintain their livelihoods.

*Change happens in response to: New Realities, Trends and Events.*

## NEW REALITIES

The **role of education** in the pursuit of employment is a new reality. Good paying jobs require more education and a well refined skill set than they did in years past. Many jobs that previously required a high school education now require a two or a four year degree. Indeed, when President Obama gave his first speech to Congress, he said that education and training after high school is no longer desirable. It is necessary. The new reality is that career success requires *lifelong learning*. You can no longer be successful if you do not remain current in your field and ready to re-train for the emerging jobs that are replacing old fields of employment.

Another new reality is that the normal age for *retirement is changing.* 72 (or older) is the new 65. Many people simply cannot afford to retire when they expected. They need to stick it out for a while or find a new job for their retirement years. Economists had for years predicted that there would be tremendous labor shortages occurring when the baby-boom generation started retiring, and that their retirements would create endless opportunities. That prediction no longer holds.

Part of the reason that retirement is changing is that now, more than ever, **you are on your own** with your career. There was a time when workers could count on their employers providing security, healthcare, education and retirement benefits. That is no longer necessarily the case. It used to be the norm that employers would provide defined benefit packages. That meant you knew exactly what you would get and that the employer would keep paying for those benefits, even if the costs went up. Now, most employers offer defined contributions. In other words, they will put a certain amount of money into providing, above and beyond salary, but when costs go up, you're responsible for the difference.

With change happening rapidly and relentlessly, the new reality is that you have to be prepared to **reinvent yourself** on a regular basis. The pace of change is accelerating and it comes in many forms: technological, social, political and economic. You could show up one day at the job you thought was stable and secure, only to find out that you've been laid off. Your job may not exist tomorrow. In fact, your industry may not exist or it may have been shipped off to another country. The new reality is that you will need to re-tool and reinvent yourself more than just once. You have to be ready when change happens, and you need to maintain **awareness** to know when it's coming.

## TRENDS

Work has become a moving target due to a myriad of factors. In the last two decades we have become all too familiar with terms that dump tens of thousands of workers out into the cold.

*Globalization*
*Buyouts*
*Downsizing*
*Restructuring*
*Mergers*
*Outsourcing*
*Right sizing*
*Offshoring*
*Disruptive technologies*
*Meltdowns*
*Recession and Depression*

All of the above can be described as trends that will impact the labor market for years at a time.

There are other trends that should have a positive effect. The buzz words here are: declining oil prices, recovery plans, stimulus packages and budget priorities.

For example: In his State of the Union address in 2015 President Obama released a budget plan that set ambitious goals in the areas of *child care, minimum wage, sick leave, community college education, science and technology, cyber security, climate change, and infrastructure.*

The outcome of these goals will fundamentally alter the employment market for years to come. Taking science and technology as an example, there will be research, development, production, public relations, sales and advertising.

The aging population will also become a part of this wave of change. As people have started traveling to obtain medical services, and recreation is recognized as a significant factor in wellness whole industries have emerged and expanded. There is a yoga studio every few blocks.

The outcome of the healthcare reform will determine whether manufacturing in America will survive. Right now, when you buy American, you may be paying more for worker benefits than you are for the product or service you are purchasing.

On the education, science and technology, and cyber security fronts, new investments will mean more jobs for university and community college teachers, more money for research, and more opportunities for workers to upgrade their skills for an advanced technology economy. If education policies advance, their will be more opportunities at home, here in the U.S., for workers in the information and service industries. With a better educated workforce here at home, employers won't be shipping high tech jobs overseas.

The climate change frontier is part of a continuing trend that is expanding rapidly: the "Greening of America." With the world having finally woken up to the threat of global warming, there will be a wide range of employment opportunities created in response to environmental demands. And they won't just be in science and technology. It also affects construction, service, transportation, manufacturing, information, finance and so on.

## EVENTS

Sometimes, the world-of-work will change dramatically in response to immediate events.

When Hurricane Katrina hit New Orleans, the economic impact was felt throughout the country. Building supplies became more expensive in Seattle. Home insurance rates went up in Sacramento. Labor costs went up in South Dakota. Even if there had not been as much devastation, gasoline prices everywhere would still have been impacted by the closing of a few refineries.

When oil prices spiked up more than 100% in 2008, there was tremendous upheaval in many industries. There were good and bad repercussions. People thought harder about their automobile choices and where they will live. They thought more about fuel economy in both decisions. Manufacturers realized that if they manufacture in China, they might lose all of the savings gained from a cheaper labor market by incurring heavy transportation costs to get their goods to market. Cheap oil allowed for inexpensive transport of goods across the globe. But once the cost of shipping a 40-foot container to the US jumped from $3000 earlier in the decade, to $8000 in 2008, things changed. And then in 2009 and again in 2015, oil prices dropped back down.

Things happen everyday that change every-

## 3.2

# AWARENESS EXERCISE

*Choose a story from today's news. Then, on a piece of paper, see if you can come up with ten things that might happen as a result of that event.*

**This was not a one time exercise!**

For the serious job seeker, this task does not end with having analyzed just one news story. Instead, it has to be a way of thinking about what's going on and what different events might mean. You don't want to be the person who goes out looking for a job as a mortgage broker while the mortgage industry is melting down.

Oil producing states and countries have learned all too well the booms and busts caused by fluctuating prices of crude.

You don't want to be the last one to know which industries are going to grow in the coming years. You don't want to miss or overlook an opportunity, or fail to consider an option because you thought it wouldn't be worth it. You don't want to train for a job that won't be there and you don't want to pass up a training opportunity because you think there won't be any jobs in that field.

Maintaining an awareness of the world around you is also going to improve your chances of landing that job that you want. When you interview, a prospective employer is going to want to know that you know their industry, that you know the trends that might affect it, and that you are alert to the forces that will shape it. An employer will want to know that you are thinking!

thing. Someone introduces a new product. Someone recalls an old one. A an oil pipeline breaks and pollutes a river or a nuclear power plant melts down. A study reports that subsidies for corn-based ethanol impact food prices. A computer battery catches on fire. A bank goes belly-up. The price of oil goes up. The price of oil goes down. A terrorist group strikes in Paris.

It can be good news or it can be bad news. Your task is to maintain awareness and to figure out what might happen next. When things happen, your task is to pay attention and to connect the dots - which industries will grow and which industries will decline.

04

# RESEARCH

## 4.0

# RESEARCHING YOUR CAREER OPTIONS: INTRODUCTION

Researching your options and exploring careers is not just about gathering information. It's about getting excited and getting yourself motivated about the possibilities. It's about understanding that there are worlds of opportunity that exist, just waiting for you to discover them.

*Here, the research focus is on using published information. Later, when we get to the job search Strategy phase, you will learn how to research your career options by going out and talking to people, using contacts and informational interviews.* Both types of research are important.

In theory, the research phase of your career plan should come after you have completed the self-assessment, after you have identified your skills and interests. But that's not how it works. The research has to start in advance of skill identification, and has to continue in an interactive fashion as part of the self-assessment process.

*We have already talked about Awareness in terms of keeping yourself informed about the world around you. Here, the task is to start developing an Awareness of the world-of-work.*

You will find that the work you do here is important when you begin to assess your skills and interests. When you begin to Focus on gathering information about yourself, you will need to constantly check to see how what you learn fits with different types of careers.

You probably already have a number of ideas about what type of job you're looking for. In order to Focus on what you really want to do, you need to find out more about the career ideas you already have in mind.

It is impossible to make decisions about what you will do with your life if you do not have information about occupations that correspond with your interests and aspirations. For any career you might consider, you need to know what a typical work day is like, what training and education is necessary, and what industries provide the best opportunities.

There are certain things that allow people to achieve success in specific careers. Different jobs require different skills, interests and temperaments. This is part of what you will be looking for as you start exploring careers.

You also need to know the working conditions for different jobs, where those careers are located, how much demand there is for those workers, what the future holds and what type of salary you should expect.

*Information is power!*

## 4.1

# RESEARCHING YOUR CAREER OPTIONS USING PUBLISHED INFORMATION ON THE WEB

*The absolute best sources for career and job information include:*

*The Occupational Outlook
Handbook (OOH)
Indeed.com
O*Net Online
Company web sites
Sal*

## OCCUPATIONAL OUTLOOK HANDBOOK

You can find tons of great information about hundreds of occupations in the OOH. I have been using it and recommending it for more than thirty years. Published by the U.S. Bureau of Labor Statistics, it used to be a set of huge books and quarterly updates. Now, of course, it's online and includes important information about different jobs, like:

- *the training and education needed*
- *earnings*
- *expected job prospects*
- *what workers do on the job*
- *working conditions*
- *information about the job market in each State*
- *information about the jobs and economy of tomorrow*

To find an occupation in the OOH, search by job titles or occupational fields. You can also enter tools or skills you might use in an occupation.

For a really long list of job titles in 23 major groups, you can visit the SOC - Standard Occupational Classifications.

## INDEED.COM

**Indeed.com** is an aggregator of job announcements and advertisements from all across the web. If all you were going to do to find work was to look at the want ads, this would either be a perfect starting point or a one-stop solution.

In addition to showing ads, Indeed.com also has salary information and job trend information. Their data comes from what's being advertised.

As you look at job announcements online, you need to understand that this is not how you are actually going to find a job, not if you are a serious job seeker. The odds are that online announcements are not going to yield a position. You need to look at them to understand the types of positions being announced and to better understand your options and to have a sense of what is happening in the employment field.

## O*NET ONLINE

This resource used to be known as the Guide to Occupational Exploration and it used to be in one book that fit neatly on a shelf. It is now an exhaustive information source that is extensively cross-referenced. On the *main search page*, you might find it useful to search in the Career Clusters, Job Families or "In-Demand Industry Clusters." The "Job Zones" describe different preparation levels.

We are going to be using this more as a reference after you have done a self-assessment of your interests. The *search by interests* page is useful in a couple of ways. It can help you understand how your interests fit with different career paths and it can lead you to job descriptions that will help you filter through what you really like and what you really don't.

The way that specific occupations are described at O*Net (with exhaustive lists of characteristics) is not as useful as the descriptions in the OOH. But when it comes time to write your resume, you want to go here to see the skill lists associated with different careers.

## COMPANY WEBSITES

Before you go on any informational interview or job interview, and before you file an application or send a resume, you absolutely need to check out the company's website.

You need to know the business they're in and whatever else you can learn about the company's mission, goals and areas of operation.

Most companies post their available jobs on their websites, but often they are just posting information about their higher level positions. If you are at the entry level, this is often really good information because the job descriptions for the executives will tell you what the people down below must be helping with.

For company websites you can search using Google.

## SALARY.COM, GLASSDOOR.COM & PAYSCALE.COM

At the start, you only need to have some general information about the salaries you might expect. When it comes time to make decisions about accepting a job offer and negotiating a salary, you want as much information as possible. The *OOH* will give you the general ranges (see the OES data), but sites such as *glassdoor.com*, *salary.com* and *payscale.com* will give you information that is specific to particular cities or zip codes and that is based on large pools of data. For most purposes, the "free reports" are sufficient. If you are negotiating for that million dollar bonus, you might consider their fee based reports. Their data comes from compensation specialists with access, and from surveys and research.

When you use these salary estimators, make certain that you look carefully at the job descriptions. You want to make certain that the job for which you are getting a salary estimate has similar duties and requirements as the one you are applying for.

## 4.2

## RESEARCH STRATEGY: TASKS & SUMMARY

*Your immediate task is to start researching careers using the Occupational Outlook Handbook. This is part of the Awareness process, learning more about the world-of-work.*

*You should also start looking at job announcements,* keeping in mind that this is only one part of the job search strategy, and often times not the most important part.

Use the search box for **indeed.com**.

*Later, when you begin to Focus, and after you've started the self-assessment, we are going to be looking at job information at O\*Net Online,* matching your interests and your career personality to specific occupations. I will be giving you a list of links at O\*Net that you will want to follow as part of your self-assessment. You will also be using this resource to help focus on the keywords describing skills that you will want to include on your resume.

*When you get started on your informational interviews and focused job-seeking, you are going to be doing a lot more research at company websites.*

*Finally, when it comes time for salary negotiations, you are going to be using salary.com and also indeed.com for your research.*

# SELF-ASSESSMENT

**5.0**

# SELF-ASSESSMENT: DON'T LEAVE HOME WITHOUT IT!

Self-assessment is a big topic. And it's the one that you probably think you can skip. But this is the heart and soul of the job search process for serious job seekers.

I know. You already know what you want to do and where you want to work and what you have to offer. But with 30+ years experience in this field, what I am telling you is that if you don't do these exercises, you are going to end up with a mediocre resume. You are not going to be prepared for interviews, you're not going to do your best when you fill out applications. And if you get an offer, you're not going to be properly prepared to negotiate that salary.

Crunch time is coming (hopefully). You're going to be sitting down for an interview and they're going to want you to be able to tell them who you are, what you know and what you have to offer. If you are not prepared to immediately describe your skills and abilities, your interests and your passions, your motivations and your aspirations, you're not going to get the job. You need to be entirely comfortable talking about why you get up in the morning, and you need to be convincing when you tell an employer why they should hire you. You also need to know if you are going to let them hire you.

That's what self-assessment is about. It involves a set of exercises that will help you know yourself and help you convey that to potential employers.

Self-assessment will help you put together your resume. It will help you list your skills and abilities on job applications. It will help you navigate the interview. When you get to the interview, you don't want to just make up the answers, When

they ask you about yourself, you want to be totally prepared to tell them who you are.

Some of these exercises will seem insubstantial. Some of them will be redundant. But you need to do each and everyone of them. Don't even think about coming to see me in my office and to seek my advice if you haven't started this process.

My very best story about the importance of self-assessment involves a young man who studied engineering and manufacturing technology. He came to me perplexed about how to find a job. He already knew what careers were available to him and what companies he should be focusing on. He said he just wanted me to tweak up his resume. He thought he knew everything about where he was going. I insisted that he do the self-assessment exercises. What I learned is that he liked to play golf. He loved playing golf more than anything else in life. Fast forward through the self-assessment and job seeking strategy: he ended up with a job with a company manufacturing golf equipment. He is an engineer with a job where he spends half of his time "testing" out equipment on the golf links!

Had he not done the exercises, I'm sure I could have placed him in a factory manufacturing widgets. But he let me know what he was passionate about, and that helped us focus his career search, and that focus landed him a job that was a perfect fit with his interests.

So here's my advice: do all of the self-assessment exercises. Get to know yourself and get to be comfortable telling people what motivates you and what you are good at.

The first exercise I want you to do has to do with your career personality.

## 5.1

# SELF-ASSESSMENT: WHAT IS YOUR CAREER PERSONALITY TYPE?

The first self-assessment task is about finding your career personality type or "Holland Code." John Holland is a psychologist who developed a "theory of careers" that is routinely used in assessing vocational interests. His view is that "the choice of a vocation is an expression of personality" and that there are six primary types. Your career personality is usually described in terms of the two or three codes that best describe you, so that means there are a lot more than just six actual types.

These personality types are not just used to describe your career interests and personality. They are also used to describe work environments and occupations. Knowing your type preferences is important to the what and where questions - what you want to do and where you want to do it.

The six primary personalities or interest profiles are:

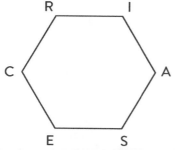

**R** EALISTIC
**I** NVESTIGATIVE
**A** RTISTIC
**S** OCIAL
**E** NTERPRISING
**C** ONVENTIONAL

They are represented on a hexagon to show that the closer they are together (next to each other and across the hexagon), the more they are related and the more similar those people are. The Conventional and Artistic types are on opposite sides and are the least alike.

No person is really just one type, and most people will identify with the characteristics of two or three types.

The Perfect Career Finder is a short survey that we will use to chart your vocational preferences and interests and to find your Holland Codes.

**FIRST** read the description of each work and personality type (see following page).

**SECOND** for each of the 15 possible pairs on the hexagon, select or circle the letter for the career type you prefer, or the one that best describes your career interests.

**THIRD** count how many times you chose each letter:

R _____
I _____
A _____
S _____
E _____
C _____

The two highest numbers represent your primary work-life preferences.

Now your task is to look at some jobs or careers that fit with your personality, your interests, your skills and your motivations.

At O*Net Online (www.onetonline.org/explore/interests) you can search careers based on your Holland Codes. At the "Interests Search" page, click on your primary interest area. Then you can add your second or third personality code to the search.

The jobs are listed in order by "job zones" - the ranking indicates how much training, education or preparation is needed for any particular job. If you click on the job title, you will see a complete description. It will tell you about the tasks and activities involved, and about the skills, knowledge and abilities required.

The purpose of this exercise is not to tell you what type of career you should pursue. The purpose is to help you explore and discover some of the job titles that fit with your interests.

TAKE THE TEST ONLINE
*OR ON THE APP*
*TO GET QUICK RESULTS*
SERIOUSJOBSEEKER.COM

## REALISTIC

- enjoy "hands-on" work using tools, equipment, and machinery like working outdoors or with plants or animals
- enjoy sports or outdoor activities like rock climbing, biking, hiking or backpacking don't like doing a lot of paperwork
- frequently work on teams to accomplish tasks or complete projects
- like building or fixing things and trouble shooting problems

## SOCIAL

- like to help people - prefer teaching, communicating, and serving others
- skilled with words - able to share ideas effectively to enlighten or inform others
- able to engage people at a personal and emotional levels
- can work with minimal structure or supervision
- tend not to be significantly money motivated
- these people are altruistic, sociable, friendly and socially responsible

## INVESTIGATIVE

- like to observe, learn, analyze, evaluate, and solve problems
- prefer working with information and data, rather than with people or things
- enjoy strategy games (chess, checkers etc) or computer games
- frequently skilled in math and/ or science may play a musical instrument - (music has a math component)
- these people tend to be analytical and may appear quiet and pensive

## ARTISTIC

- enjoy working in unstructured situations using imagination and creativity
- tend to dislike having to follow rules or set procedures
- enjoy doing things that requiring a sense of design and an appreciation of aesthetics
- these people are frequently innovators who tend to "think way outside the box"

## ENTERPRISING

- skilled at persuading, leading, performing, influencing or managing others
- able to work to meet organizational goals or for economic gain
- highly money motivated
- work requires energy and ambition, and a fair amount of self-confidence
- jobs are usually business related and often involve sales and promotion
- entrepreneurial, energetic and optimistic; establish rapport easily - sociable and talkative
- these people are focused on competing and getting ahead

## CONVENTIONAL

- prefer work that is detailed and orderly, structured and routine
- enjoy work that involves data and information, rather than people or things
- like structure with rules that are known
- dislike having to be creative
- jobs in this area involve orderly processes and record keeping
- these people are reliable, efficient, conforming, and conscientious individuals

# CAREER PERSONALITY SELF-ASSESSMENT
## *THE PERFECT CAREER FINDER*

**For each pair, circle the career type that you prefer or that best describes your career interests**

## R
### REALISTIC
Practical hands on work, using tools, building things, operating machines.

## I
### INVESTIGATIVE
Solving problems using ideas and information, analyzing data, observing and learning, applying science.

## C
### CONVENTIONAL
Detailed and orderly work that is structured and routine, following set procedures, often with numbers and data.

## S
### SOCIAL
Helping people to learn or to solve problems, teaching, communicating, serving to make things better.

## E
### ENTERPRISING
Persuading, leading, motivating and influencing people for economic gain or to meet organization goals; selling.

## R
### REALISTIC
Practical hands on work, using tools, building things, operating machines.

## A
### ARTISTIC
Creative, unstructured and expressive work, often involving design and aesthetics.

## I
### INVESTIGATIVE
Solving problems using ideas and information, analyzing data, observing and learning, applying science.

## E
### ENTERPRISING
Persuading, leading, motivating and influencing people for economic gain or to meet organization goals, selling.

## C
### CONVENTIONAL
Detailed and orderly work that is structured and routine, following set procedures, often with numbers and data.

## R
### REALISTIC
Practical hands on work, using tools, building things, operating machines.

## A
### ARTISTIC
Creative, unstructured and expressive work, often involving design and aesthetics.

## I
### INVESTIGATIVE
Solving problems using ideas and information, analyzing data, observing and learning, applying science.

## S
### SOCIAL
Helping people to learn or to solve problems, teaching, communicating, serving to make things better.

## C
### CONVENTIONAL
Detailed and orderly work that is structured and routine, following set procedures, often with numbers and data.

## R
### REALISTIC
Practical hands on work, using tools, building things, operating machines.

## S
### SOCIAL
Helping people to learn or to solve problems, teaching, communicating, serving to make things better.

## A
### ARTISTIC
Creative, unstructured and expressive work, often involving design and aesthetics.

## E
### ENTERPRISING
Persuading, leading, motivating and influencing people for economic gain or to meet organization goals, selling.

## I
### INVESTIGATIVE
Solving problems using ideas and information, analyzing data, observing and learning, applying science.

## R

### REALISTIC

Practical hands on work, using tools, building things, operating machines.

## S

### SOCIAL

Helping people to learn or to solve problems, teaching, communicating, serving to make things better.

## A

### ARTISTIC

Creative, unstructured and expressive work, often involving design and aesthetics.

## E

### ENTERPRISING

Persuading, leading, motivating and influencing people for economic gain or to meet organization goals, selling.

## I

### INVESTIGATIVE

Solving problems using ideas and information, analyzing data, observing and learning, applying science.

## C

### CONVENTIONAL

Detailed and orderly work that is structured and routine, following set procedures, often with numbers and data.

## S

### SOCIAL

Helping people to learn or to solve problems, teaching, communicating, serving to make things better.

## E

### ENTERPRISING

Persuading, leading, motivating and influencing people for economic gain or to meet organization goals, selling.

## A

### ARTISTIC

Creative, unstructured and expressive work, often involving design and aesthetics.

## C

### CONVENTIONAL

Detailed and orderly work that is structured and routine, following set procedures, often with numbers and data.

Realistic = _____   Investigative = _____   Artistic = _____   Social = _____   Enterprising = _____   Conventional = _____

Top 2 scores: _____ & _____

**5.2**

# SELF-ASSESSMENT:
## *SKILLS ASSESSMENT INTRODUCTION*

**Skills are the basic building blocks of jobs.**
While it is certain that you have many skills and many talents, you need to identify those that make you someone an employer will want to hire. You need to be able to describe them in a way that will make an employer want to hire you and make them understand that you are the best candidate for the job.

You also need to clearly understand your skill set so that you can focus on finding the job that is just right for you.

*There are some skills you have that you probably have no interest in using as part of your daily work.* What you need to identify are those skills that you prefer using (your preferred skills) and those that you are motivated to use (your motivated skills). It is certain that you have skills that you find to be a drudge to apply and others that bring you satisfaction and enjoyment.

*Skills develop early in life and throughout life.* Most of your **motivated skills** have served you in a variety of situations. Those skills have been refined by life experiences like sports, clubs, and hobbies, or even just hanging around working on the car with a parent or another adult. They provided enjoyment when you were a child, and as an adult, they will help you get what you want and what you need out of life. The ones we need to identify are those that have provided you with a sense of accomplishment.

*Many of your skills are "transferable" and can be applied in a range of situations.* These are skills that you have been using since you were a little kid. Think about it. There were kids in your grammar school class who were the leaders: the class president or team captain. There were also enterprising kids who could sell more tickets or cookies than anyone else. There was the artist who could draw fabulously in third grade. And there was the writer who could spin an incredible tale for a writing assignment. Some were great communicators, never afraid to stand up and read their reports. Some were great at fixing things or building things. And remember the kid who always took notes and made sure that every detail on a group project was attended to?

*When we looked at your career personality type, we were looking at your motivated skills and interests in a general sort of way. Now we need to drill down and focus on your skill set in a more specific fashion.*

We need to be able to describe your skills in a way that will allow you to translate them into specific career choices and to communicate your interest in using those skills to an employer.

For this, we are going to do a few different exercises. We are going to review your skills in terms of what you are good at and in terms of how you have exercised those skills relative to past accomplishments. This is not just a matter of your being able to look at a job description and saying "I can do that and I can do that too." This is a matter of understanding what you really want to do and having the confidence to look an employer in the eye and tell her that you are the best candidate for the job.

## 5.3

# SELF-ASSESSMENT:
## *SKILL ASSESSMENT EXERCISES, 3 TASKS TO COMPLETE*

*To make this work, you need to do all of the skill assessment exercises! And it is best to do them in order:*

### 01. MOTIVATED SKILLS INVENTORY

### 02. TYING SKILLS TO ACCOMPLISHMENTS

### 03. FINDING SKILLS IN YOUR ACCOMPLISHMENTS

All skill assessments are available online for fast & automatic results.
seriousjobseeker.com

## 01. MOTIVATED SKILLS INVENTORY

For each skill, you are going to give two ratings:
* how much of that skill do you possess?
* how motivated are you to use that skill?

Skills are rated from 1 to 4.
Your motivation to use each skill is rated from zero to 3.

### SKILL LEVEL

1 =     Little or no skill
2 =     Some basic ability
3 =     Generally well skilled
4 =     Advanced skill level

### MOTIVATION LEVEL

0 =     Not motivated to use this skill
1 =     Motivated to use this skill if necessary
2 =     Generally enjoy using this skill
3 =     Really enjoy using this skill

For each skill area listed, rate your ability level and your motivation, and then add the two numbers together.

Focus on your 7s!

A skill rating of 7 means you are highly skilled and highly motivated.

A score of 6 means you are either highly skilled and generally motivated, or that you are highly motivated and generally well skilled. These areas represent viable options.

Scores of 5 and below describe areas in which you have either less skill or less motivation. You may have some ambivalence about a career that requires you to apply that ability.

Skills you rate at 4, 3 or 2 are not at the top of your list.

A score of 1 means you have little skill and no motivation.

After you identify your motivated skills, underline or highlight the words or terms that specifically apply to your skill set. These are words and phrases that you will be using in the next exercise and when you construct your resume.

## COMMUNICATION SKILLS

*WRITING*: Possess good to excellent writing skills. Able to create business or technical documents, correspondence, and other effective written communications. Enjoy creative writing.
*Skill level ___ + Motivation ___ = ___*

*SPEAKING*: Comfortable speaking in meetings and communicating complex information in an easily understandable form to individuals at various levels. *Skill level ___ + Motivation ___ = ___*

PRESENTATION: Skilled at giving presentations to large or small groups. Able to develop effective visual aids for presentations.
*Skill level* ___ + *Motivation* ___ = ___

PERSUADING: Comfortable using persuasive skills to convince others as to a particular course of action. *Skill level* ___ + *Motivation* ___ = ___

SELLING: Skilled at convincing others to buy a product or service.
*Skill level* ___ + *Motivation* ___ = ___

DRAMATICS: Enjoy delivering information, ideas or stories dramatically.
*Skill level* ___ + *Motivation* ___ = ___

NEGOTIATING: Capable of bargaining with others to reach a desired agreement.
*Skill level* ___ + *Motivation* ___ = ___

## MARKETING, PUBLIC RELATIONS, AND CUSTOMER SERVICE SKILLS

SOCIAL EASE: Effective in social situations; comfortable meeting new people and establish rapport easily. *Skill level* ___ + *Motivation* ___ = ___

PUBLIC RELATIONS: Interact effectively on a continual basis with customers requiring information, service or help.
*Skill level* ___ + *Motivation* ___ = ___

CUSTOMER/USER SERVICE: Skilled at listening carefully to customer needs and complaints. Able to identify, troubleshoot and resolve problems to customer 's satisfaction. Skilled at defusing customer anger or frustration; able to create a positive experience for the customer.
*Skill level* ___ + *Motivation* ___ = ___

MARKETING AND SALES: Skilled at identifying customer needs and preferences and making appropriate product or service recommendations.
*Skill level* ___ + *Motivation* ___ = ___

PROFESSIONAL IMAGE: Able to present a good professional appearance. Able to represent an organization effectively in a positive light. Enjoy dressing appropriately for professional situations. Project a solid professional image.
*Skill level* ___ + *Motivation* ___ = ___

PERFORMANCE IMPROVEMENT: Able to deal effectively with objective criticism or feedback and improve performance. Able to identify areas of deficiency to improve performance. Able to defuse problems and resolve complaints with positive action.
*Skill level* ___ + *Motivation* ___ = ___

QUANTITATIVE ANALYSIS SKILLS: Computational Speed Able to process, compute or manipulate numerical data rapidly and accurately with or without the aid of a calculator or computing device. *Skill level* ___ + *Motivation* ___ = ___

WORK WITH NUMERICAL DATA: Skilled at dealing with and manipulating large amounts of quantitative data. Able to compile, interpret, and present complex data.
*Skill level* ___ + *Motivation* ___ = ___

SOLVE QUANTITATIVE PROBLEMS: Able to analyze numerical data using complex equations and methods to arrive at a satisfactory solution. Able to recommend course of action based on quantitative analysis.
*Skill level* ___ + *Motivation* ___ = ___

COMPUTER SKILLS: Able to analyze customer hardware or software needs or problems. Skilled at writing software specifications and developing computer software programs or software systems in order to automate processes for maximum efficiency and data collection. Able to identify hard-

ware solutions based on careful analysis.
*Skill level ___  +  Motivation ___  =  ___*

## ANALYTICAL - RESEARCH SKILLS

**SCIENTIFIC CURIOSITY:** Significant interest in scientific phenomena. Motivated to explore, research, pursue and develop new technologies and innovations. *Skill level ___  +  Motivation ___  =  ___*

**RESEARCH:** Able to gather information, in a systematic way, for a particular field of knowledge, verifying facts or principles.
*Skill level ___  +  Motivation ___  =  ___*

**TECHNICAL WORK:** Able to understand and use engineering, or industrial principles, tools and equipment to improve processes, services or products. *Skill level ___  +  Motivation ___  =  ___*

## TECHNICAL REASONING

**MECHANICAL REASONING:** Able to understand the ways that hardware, machinery or tools operate and the relationships between mechanical operations.
*Skill level ___  +  Motivation ___  =  ___*

**SPATIAL REASONING:** Possess excellent spatial reasoning, able to judge the relationship of objects in space. Able to judge shapes and sizes of objects and manipulate them digitally or mentally and analyze the effects.
*Skill level ___  +  Motivation ___  =  ___*

**OUTDOOR WORK:** Enjoy working outdoors on construction, environmental or landscape projects, to manage operations or to gather technical information or environmental data.
*Skill level ___  +  Motivation ___  =  ___*

**TROUBLESHOOTING AND PROBLEM SOLVING:** Skilled with analyzing mechanical, electrical, software or hardware problems and coming up with effective solutions.
*Skill level ___  +  Motivation ___  =  ___*

## CREATIVITY AND INNOVATION

**ARTISTIC:** Possess excellent artistic abilities. Able to create drawings, paintings or stories using imagination. Able to use color and shapes to create visually pleasing images in one or many forms including computer images or in more traditional media. Able to create new ideas and forms with various physical objects.
*Skill level ___  +  Motivation ___  =  ___*

**CREATIVE OR IMAGINATIVE WITH IDEAS:** Using imagination, able to create new ideas, projects, or programs. Able to conceive existing elements in new ways.
*Skill level ___  +  Motivation ___  =  ___*

## TEACHING, TRAINING, INSTRUCTING OR COUNSELING

**TEACHING:** Able to explain complex ideas, concepts, or principles in an easily understandable fashion. Able to provide knowledge or insight to individuals or groups.
*Skill level ___  +  Motivation ___  =  ___*

**COACHING:** Able to assist an individual on improving his or her performance in a specific subject or skill area.
*Skill level ___  +  Motivation ___  =  ___*

**COUNSELING:** Able to listen and sort out details and information and give advice or counsel, while engaging in a helping/supportive relationship with an individual who is experiencing distress. *Skill level ___  +  Motivation ___  =  ___*

## PROJECT MANAGEMENT - LEADERSHIP - MOTIVATION SKILLS

### MANAGEMENT AND SUPERVISION:

Management and Supervision: Skilled at effectively overseeing, managing or directing the work of others. Able to motivate individuals to perform at their peak level. Able to lead teams, and manage resources effectively. Skilled at managing projects, establishing time lines, meeting deadlines, and delivering high quality products and services. Able to maintain a positive working environment, empowering employees to produce a high quality product or service. Comfortable working with individuals at all levels of authority.

*Skill level* ___ + *Motivation* ___ = ___

### PLANNING:

*PLANNING:* Able to plan and develop a program, project or set of ideas through organized and systematic preparation and arrangement of tasks, activities and schedules. Able to coordinate people and resources to put a plan into effect and meet specific deadlines.

*Skill level* ___ + *Motivation* ___ = ___

### ORGANIZATION:

*ORGANIZATION:* Arranging people, data or objects in a systematic fashion to allow for the effective use of time and resources;. Organizing information to allow for easy access.

*Skill level* ___ + *Motivation* ___ = ___

### DETAIL MANAGEMENT:

*DETAIL MANAGEMENT:* Able to work with a great variety and/or volume of information without losing track of any items in the total situation. Comfortable managing small detail oriented tasks that are part of the larger project.

*Skill level* ___ + *Motivation* ___ = ___

### DECISION MAKING:

*DECISION MAKING:* Comfortable making judgments or reaching conclusions about matters which require specific action. Able to accept the responsibility for and the consequences of such actions. *Skill level* ___ + *Motivation* ___ = ___

ONLINE VERSION
*SERIOUSJOBSEEKER.COM*

# 02. TYING SKILLS TO ACCOMPLISHMENTS

Now that you have identified your skills, you need to be able to tell an employer how you have demonstrated that skill in a real life situation. An employer might say: "So you say that you are good at project management. Give me an example of a situation where you have used that skill". Or "Describe to me an accomplishment you feel good about where you demonstrated this skill."

Your next move is to "own" your skills. You need to search your memory for experiences that you can recall to backup your ownership of a particular skill. The accomplishments do not necessarily have to be from your work experience. They can come from any part of your life.

When an employer considers you for a job, they are not necessarily looking for experience directly tied to their industry or even the available position. They are looking for "indicators of potential". They are looking for a skill set. If you can demonstrate that you already have the skills necessary to be successful in the position you are interviewing for, they will hire you.

What are employers looking for? Employers are looking for the same things they have always looked for. They are looking for talented individuals who match their technical needs and who fit into their organizational structure.

## HERE ARE YOUR INSTRUCTIONS:

On a sheet of paper, or in your word processor, write down each of the skills that you underlined or highlighted on the Motivated Skills Inventory page.

When you copy the skill descriptions here, you do not need to write them down exactly as they appeared on the list. What you want to do is to start constructing short, declarative statements describing your particular skills.

After you have listed your skills, think about what you have done in the past to demonstrate that skill and write down a description of that accomplishment.

These skill descriptions are part of the material you will use later for your resume.

## HERE IS AN EXAMPLE:

| SKILL | ACCOMPLISHMENT |
| --- | --- |
| *Planning:* Able to plan and develop a program or project, on time and under budget, meeting goals and objectives. | Boy Scout/Eagle Scout project: designed and built a play yard for neighborhood child care center. |
| *Teaching:* Able to explain complex ideas, concepts, or principles in an easily understandable fashion. | Tutored high school math students. |
| *Creative or Imaginative with Ideas*: Using imagination, able to create new ideas, projects, or programs. | Developed a community garden for a neighborhood grammar school. |

They are looking for people who have good interpersonal skills, get along with other people, communicate effectively, and who can demonstrate that they have the right stuff: the team, leadership, organization, and problem solving skills that get things done.

Employers want to know that you can do the job they need to have done. They also want to know that you are motivated to do the job. Often times, they will hire an enthusiastic inexperienced candidate over an experienced candidate. Your job is to convince them that you have the necessary skills and that you are motivated to use them.

This *Skill/Accomplishment* list is something you want to spend a fair amount of time working on. After you have written it the first time, you need to continue to zoom in on the precise skill statements that might go on your resume.

Zooming in: Let's look at the "planning" skill.

On the Skills Inventory, "planning" started as: Able to plan and develop a program, project or set of ideas through organized and systematic preparation and arrangement of tasks, activities and schedules.

In the example above, it became: Able to plan and develop a program or project.

For your resume, the skill statement could become:

Skilled at project management.
*or:*
Able to plan, manage and deliver complex programs and projects.
*or:*
Experienced developing, planning and coordinating large scale projects and events.
*or:*
Able to schedule tasks and activities for large groups engaged in complex projects.

Your skills assessment does not end here!

Until your resume is complete, your interviews are done and your salary negotiations are finished, you are going to continue to work on describing your skills and accomplishments and preparing to present them in a clear and concise manner. The more you work on this task, the more confident you will feel as you move forward, and the more convincing you will be in your self-presentation.

The next task is to take a look at some of your accomplishments and to see what skills you have put to use and felt good about using.

# 03. FINDING SKILLS IN YOUR ACCOMPLISHMENTS

We've looked at your motivated skills by going through an inventory where you rated them in a few different ways. And you've made a list of past accomplishments where you have demonstrated those skills.

But you may have other skills that we've overlooked or that you didn't think to highlight. What we need to do next is to look at some of your accomplishments and see what skills you displayed in the course of those experiences.

Yes, it seems like we're going over the same ground again. But as I said before, you need to feel confident when you present yourself on your resume and in interviews. You need to be prepared! This will help.

---

## HERE ARE THE INSTRUCTIONS:

---

1. *Make a list of about five to seven accomplishments you feel good about.* These can be experiences from any facet of your life, not necessarily work or education related. It could be something you did like planning a surprise party, finishing your senior project, becoming a U.S. citizen, organizing a charity event, planting a garden, installing a new air conditioner in your house, or taking a hike up Half Dome in Yosemite Valley. Anything you did that you feel good about.

2. *Select one or two accomplishments from your list that you would like to write a short narrative about.* Be sure to select ones that have a beginning and an end and that can be written about in just a page or two.

*Now write a page or two describing exactly what you did to make your accomplishment happen.* Begin by writing a few thoughts on a sheet of paper. When you've jotted down a few thoughts that you can use as an outline, you can write the rest of the story on your computer. (e.g.: Planning a surprise party: The first step I took was to make sure she didn't have the slightest clue that there was a party waiting for her. In order to do so, I had to create a diversion by. I had to invite all of our close friends and family, so I found her address book and ...). *Here's an example of an Accomplishment Narrative (on the next page)*

3. *For the next step, have a friend or your career coach help you.* Read the narrative out loud and have your friend jot down any thoughts they

have about the skills or abilities you used to succeed in the accomplishment. It works best if you read each sentence and brainstorm together to identify what it was necessary for you to do to make each part of it happen. If you can't think of any skills that were necessary for each step, you can refer back to the Skills Inventory we worked on before.

4. *For the last step, look at the notes your friend jotted down from your accomplishment narrative and turn them into skill statements, just like you did in the previous exercises.*

We've come to the end of the skill assessment exercises!

But we haven't finished with self-assessment. You have catalogued your motivated skills, tied your skills to accomplishments, and searched for skills in your accomplishments.

Before that, we looked at your career personality. Now we have to start looking at what motivates you in life: what you value, what really interests you and what you need to thrive.

## ACCOMPLISHMENT NARRATIVE: ▶

### DAY HIKE IN DESOLATION IN AUGUST

*An accomplishment I feel good about was my first hiking trip in Desolation Valley.*

*After becoming interested in hiking and deciding I would enjoy a trek in Desolation, I read about the area. I also got two friends interested in going along.*

*Before the hike, I decided I would have to get into shape, so we took short hikes at Pt. Reyes and in the Golden Gate Sea Shore area.*

*I spoke to people from the California Alpine Club about the best areas in Desolation, about weather conditions, and what to bring along in the way of clothing and food. I reviewed maps and checked into the types of terrain we would encounter. And then, I arranged for time off from work.*

*The hike itself would require a ferry ride across Echo Lakes, so I called for a schedule of departures and reservations. We arrived at Tahoe two days before we planned our hike. We spent one day adjusting to the altitude. The day before the*

*hike I got together last minute items: a first aid kit, peanuts, chocolate and raisins for quick energy, sandwiches, apples, sweaters, swimsuits and a Sierra cup.*

*The day of the hike we got up early, ate breakfast, gathered our things, and drove to Echo. The ferry deposited us at the trailhead with instructions for summoning it for the return trip. We hiked approximately five miles in and five miles out. After I got past being tired, I thoroughly enjoyed the hike.*

*I learned during the hike that it was wise to carry your own water into Desolation since there is little fast running water in mid to late summer and it is just not safe to drink from natural sources.*

## SKILLS FOUND IN THE NARRATIVE:

identifying interests
making decisions
analyzing information
communicating with others effectively
persuading others
selling ideas
setting goals
taking on challenges
gathering information
researching written sources
finding experts
asking questions
sharing information in easily understandable language
making lists
making arrangements
reading maps
sharing ideas
seeking advice
planning events
managing details
following instructions
troubleshooting problems

# 06

# MORE SELF-ASSESMENT

## 6.0

# MORE SELF ASSESSMENT: GETTING WHAT YOU WANT OUT OF LIFE!

The rest of the puzzle ...

Figuring out *what* you want to do and *where* you want to work is a complex task. It involves answering a variety of questions about what you need to thrive and what you want out of life.

*We have already looked at your career personality.* Your Holland Code tells us in a general way what types of work tasks interest you and what type of work environments meet your demands. Knowing your Holland Code is essential if you want to use job classification systems to find out what types of careers fit with your interests.

*We have also taken a careful and extensive inventory of your skills and your motivated skills.* The skill descriptions you developed will help you match your interests with the demands associated with specific jobs. And perhaps more importantly, you now have those skills listed in a way that will help as you build your resume and present yourself in interviews. You are ready to tell prospective employers what you can do.

*But there is still more work to be done to make certain that you know what you are looking for and to make certain that you find it. You still have to answer the "What" and the "Where" questions. You need to be clear about what you want to do and where you want to do it.*

Many of the skills you have are transferable. You can use them in a number of different industries. You need to know which industries you want to focus on.

In deciding *where* you want to apply your skills and who you will allow to employ you, you need to consider your work values and priorities. What type of work environment suits you best? What type of people do you want to work with? What should your salary and benefit expectations include? Do you need to live in a city or would you be happier somewhere else? *What really motivates you?*

In the same way that you have different skills that can be applied to different situations, you also have an inventory of acquired knowledge that spans many different areas and interests. Which knowledge areas do you want to apply to your work in order to thrive? Is it just what you learned in college or do you want to apply the knowledge you've obtained from hobbies and extracurricular pursuits? Do you have expertise in some area unrelated to your studies and training? Is it important to you to use that knowledge?

And what about lifestyle preferences? I know young attorneys, accountants and engineers who are happy working 80 hour weeks most of the year, then vacationing large at the end of the year. That might not be your style. Perhaps it's more important to you to drop your kids off at school in the morning and to pick them up in the afternoon. Maybe you like to be home for dinner, or maybe you like staring at your computer screen until you drop.

At some point, there are going to be trade-offs and compromises to consider. And there will be decisions to be made. You need to understand what is really important to you.

*There are five exercises you need to complete before you set out on the task of implementing your job search strategy.* And keep in mind that someone wanting to hire you might very well ask if you have given any thought to these issues.

You need to know what you need to be satisfied, to thrive and to get what you want out of life. At some point, you are going to allow someone to hire you. On the other side of the equation, an employer is going to want to know that the job they are offering is going to motivate and satisfy you. You are going to expect them to provide you with more training. They will want to know that they are making a good investment.

*Here are the next steps in the self-assessment process:*

| 01 | Identifying Your Work Values and Your Work Priorities |
| 02 | Inventorying and Identifying Your Key Knowledge Areas |
| 03 | Identifying Your Interest Areas |
| 04 | Identifying Your Ideal Life/ Work Environment |
| 05 | Setting Your Goals and Priorities |

## 6.1

# IDENTIFYING YOUR WORK VALUES & YOUR WORK PRIORITIES

Work satisfaction is a function of individual needs, values and priorities. Before you make career decisions, you need to identify what you need to thrive. This exercise will help you think about what is important to you in the work environment. Different things will be important at different stages in your career. What is important to you right now? What should you be looking for?

Here, you are trying to identify your most important values. After you rate each item, make a list of the 3s and then put them into rank order. Which are your most important values?

*What do you need to be satisfied with your work?*

Fill this out as if your life depended on it!

0 =     Unimportant
1 =     Somewhat Important
2 =     Very Important
3 =     Absolutely Required

Using the scale above, rate each item: How important it is to you for you to be satisfied with your work?

*Creativity:* A job in which I can develop new products, ideas or processes, or in which I can express myself. ____

*Challenge:* A demanding job which requires that I solve difficult problems. ____

*Variety:* A job that allows me to perform many different tasks. ____

*Flexibility:* A job that allows me to set my own schedule and change my working style as I wish.

____

*Learning:* A job in which I can learn and enhance my skills and abilities. ____

*Intensity:* A job that requires much time and attention, sustained effort and intense concentration. ____

*Consistency:* A job in which my duties are clearly defined and my responsibilities are stable and predictable. ____

*Independence:* A job in which I can do things my own way and make my own decisions.

____

*Teamwork*: A job in which I can work closely with a number of other individuals. ____

*Leadership*: A job in which I can lead, supervise and influence others. ____

*Job Security*: A job that I know I will be able to keep as long as I want. ____

*Stability*: A job with a solid, stable, established and predictable organization. ____

*Financial Security*: A job that provides adequately for my needs, allowing me to live comfortably. ____

*High Paying*: A job in which I can earn a good deal of money. ____

*Financial Growth*: A job that allows for continuing salary growth and opportunity. ____

*Career Growth*: A job that promises advancement, opportunity and increasing responsibility. ____

*Prestige*: A job that is important and for which others might look up to me. ____

*Support*: A job working for someone I admire and respect and to whose success I can contribute.

____

*Respect*: A job in which my work is recognized and applauded and where I feel valued as a person. ____

*Public Service*: A job in which allows me to make the world a better or safer place to live.

____

## 6.2

# INVENTORYING AND IDENTIFYING YOUR KEY KNOWLEDGE AREAS

You probably learned quite a lot by the time you graduated from college. And if you have been in the career world for any length of time, you are probably an expert in a number of fields. It is expected that you will have received additional training during the course of your career. And you have certainly learned from your experiences. Learning and the acquisition of knowledge is a life-long task, a task to be ignored only at the risk of peril to your career prospects and career success.

*The point of this exercise is to take an inventory of your knowledge base and to identify the learned elements that you are interested in using as you move forward in your career.* Some of what you know represents foundational learning. It is the basis of your skill set and your ability to learn more. Some of what you know and have learned represents knowledge that you can directly apply.

*Identifying the knowledge elements you wish to directly apply in your next (or first) career move is essential to identifying the businesses, industries or government agencies where you will seek employment.*

*The task here is to make a list of the knowledge you have acquired:*

**from formal education**
**from work experience**
**and from your general life experiences**

*More specifically, the task is to identify the knowledge you have that you want to apply in your career.*

# KNOWLEDGE INVENTORY

*Knowledge that I have acquired through formal education: (Examples: creative writing, critical thinking, city planning, political economy, marketing fundamentals, public finance, programming, motivation theory, psychology, foundation design, environmental policy, technical writing)*

| | |
|---|---|
| 1 | |
| 2 | |
| 3 | |
| 4 | |
| 5 | |

*Knowledge that I have acquired through work experience: (Examples: writing memos, working independently and in teams, time management and project organization, and technical experience)*

| | |
|---|---|
| 1 | |
| 2 | |
| 3 | |
| 4 | |
| 5 | |

*Knowledge that I have acquired through professional associations, hobbies, sports, family, clubs, life experience, etc.: (Examples: Automotive repair, audio/video installation, computer graphics, animation, team work, woodworking, music, meeting planning, golf, baseball, building construction)*

| | |
|---|---|
| 1 | |
| 2 | |
| 3 | |
| 4 | |
| 5 | |

ONLINE VERSION
SERIOUSJOBSEEKER.COM

There is probably a lot you know that you don't care to use. *The question here is: what knowledge have you acquired that to you want to apply?*

## 6.3

# FINDING LIFE INTERESTS & PURSUING YOUR PASSION

*Identifying your interests is a critical step in finding a job and finding your place in life. You probably have a lot of interests that you think are entirely unrelated to your career preferences.* We are all interested in things but think: "That can't be my day job, I can't make money doing that!"

*Well maybe that could be your day job, or maybe your day job could be something related to what you really love and are really passionate about.*

I've already told you my favorite story about a young mechanical engineer whose passion in life was playing golf. He didn't think that he needed to do any of these self-assessment exercises. His plan was just to find a job as a mechanical engineer. When we looked at his motivated skills, we found that he had excellent design skills and that design is what he wanted to do. After we completed the interest survey, I advised him to start researching companies that use mechanical engineers to design golf equipment. And he ended up working for Karsten Manufacturing in Phoenix, Arizona. He ended up designing golf equipment and spending a fair amount of time testing out their equipment on the golf links.

What helped him nail the job was the fact that the company he focused on realized that he wasn't just bringing a set of skills. He was bringing a passion for the product and the industry.

*Let me share another example.* I met with an accountant who was completely bored working in an accounting/consulting firm. He made good money but couldn't stand the work. He was interested in cars. He loved cars! He did the work necessary in identifying his skills and his interests, started searching, and ended up as the accounting manager for a high end Sacramento automobile dealership 25 years ago and now he is the CFO. That's where he belonged and where he could thrive.

Sales and marketing jobs are particularly ripe for linking skills and interests. You know when you go into a store whether or not the person is really interested in the product. I recently bought a new camera at a large electronics store. I had some questions that were answered by two different sales people. I still wasn't certain which camera to choose, and started to think that maybe I wasn't ready to buy one at all. A third salesperson asked if he could help me, and I could tell right away that he didn't just know everything about the different cameras. He knew everything about photography and wanted me to be as interested as he was! He wasn't necessarily doing what he wanted career wise, but he was working with exactly the things that interested him, sharing his passion and his knowledge with others.

*The list of examples is endless.* And it doesn't matter what your interests are. It could be cars or golf, video games, traveling, food, art, biking, hiking, police shows, fashion, mystery novels, sewing, painting, electronics, music ... whatever. The Lego company is now releasing a series of building kits based on famous architectural landmarks. That project was started by an architect who happened to be a Lego fan.

# FINDING LIFE INTERESTS & PURSUING YOUR PASSION

This exercise is simple and fun and meant to help you focus on interests that you might not ordinarily have thought about as the basis for a career opportunity. The idea is to spend some time thinking about what you really like to spend your time doing, and to think about how your education, experience and skills might be used in an industry that is aligned with your interests.

| | *Start by making a list of your favorite things and favorite activities. Make your list at least seven items long to make sure you've considered everything that interests you.* |
|---|---|
| 1 | |
| 2 | |
| 3 | |
| 4 | |
| 5 | |
| 6 | |
| 7 | |

Now go back and underline or highlight the activities or interests that you would most like to make a part of your career path ... and don't assume that it's not possible. This is not the time to be thinking about whether or not you can make money in some way related to your interests.

Later, we are going to be looking at how you can use your skills in relation to your interests. For now, let me just give you one more example:

*Music is a really common interest and it's where people typically talk about "not giving up my day job." But think about it for a moment. There are people in the music industry who have the talent and the skill. They are the artists. But there are also the people who do the publicity and public relations. There are people who do the accounting. There are sales people and sales managers. The music industry requires technicians and engineers, building and designing the equipment, training those who will use it, and actually working in the studios and theaters operating the equipment. There have to be managers of all types for people and facilities. And there are attorneys dealing with contracts and intellectual property. The music industry also needs writers. They need caterers and travel agents. They need investment specialists and some times real estate professionals. And certainly there is a need in the music industry for therapists and substance abuse counselors.*

If you think about this one industry, you will find that there are people using the skills and motivations that are associated with each and every career personality type that we looked at when we discussed the Holland Codes.

ONLINE VERSION
SERIOUSJOBSEEKER.COM

6.4

# IDENTIFYING YOUR IDEAL LIFE / WORK ENVIRONMENT

We've already looked at your work values and work priorities, the things that are important for you to experience satisfaction in your career. We've also looked at the things you've learned, the key knowledge areas that you want to apply in your work. And, we've looked at what really interests you in life. When we did the skill assessment exercises, we took an inventory of your motivated skills and how you have used them in your past accomplishments.

All of the above information is essential for answering the *What* and *Where* questions, but there is still more for you to think about as you decide where you want to work. Where is not just a matter of what company or organization you want to work for. It also includes "location, location, location" and the lifestyle you want to maintain. The question really is What are your preferences?

I have a family member who lives in Texas and who works in the oil services industry. He thinks Houston is like heaven on earth. There are good schools for his kids and a local park with a swimming pool. It never snows and it's warm there all year. Houston is a metropolis with major sports, recreation and entertainment. The country is as flat as can be and absolutely ideal for biking. If you like to eat beef, there's plenty of it. In his job, he's on the road all the time and constantly connected to the office via a smart-phone. He travels the world regularly to places most people rarely hear of, except when there are wars or revolutions. His co-workers are high energy achievers who ex-

pect everyone to take on substantial responsibility, making important decisions on a daily basis and working without a net.

My view of his work-life environment is quite different. To me, Houston is a flat, dense, and teeming metropolis, always on the move and with no escape from the oppressive heat and humidity. I like to be home at night and to turn off my cell phone. I don't mind that you can't go to the swimming pool in December. I like to hike in the mountains and go to the beach, and to have them close at hand. I don't mind making difficult decisions, but when I do, I don't want to be out there on my own without support. I hate jumping on airplanes, and when I travel, I want it to be for vacation. I like the people around me to be relaxed and reflective.

Our lifestyle goals and preferences are quite different.

For this exercise, there are three questions to answer. For each, you need to look at the positives and the negatives. Make sure you look at it to see examples of some of the things you might consider!

**01. LOCATION/LIFESTYLE -**
What do you need in a location to thrive?

**02. PEOPLE -**
What qualities do you need in the people you work with?

**03. WORK CONDITIONS -**
What do you need in your work environment to thrive?

ONLINE VERSION
SERIOUSJOBSEEKER.COM

# IDENTIFYING YOUR IDEAL LIFE/WORK ENVIRONMENT

*Location/Lifestyle* - What do you need in a location to thrive? What would you find intolerable?

*Examples:*
• small town, big city
• affordable housing, fancy housing
• short commute, commute doesn't matter
• opera, museums, classical music venues, jazz clubs, major league sports
• close to family, far from family
• schools for kids, parks, bike trails, hiking trails, close to beach, skiing
• city experience with dense housing, suburban experience, rural environment
• cold weather, hot weather, don't mind if it rains or snows
• a college or university to continue studies
• cultural diversity and cultural associations, a welcoming religious community
• red state/blue state politics
• coffee houses, fine dining, fast food, great pizza, bookstores, shopping malls

*People* - What qualities do you need in the people you work with? What would you find intolerable?

*Examples:*
• friendly and engaging people who help and support you with your work
• people who stick to themselves and leave you alone to do your own work
• people who are competent, smart, ambitious, lazy, intolerant, overbearing, uncooperative, neat, sloppy, fun, resentful, opinionated
• people who like to socialize and involve you in family and off-the-job activities, people who have their own lives away from work
• people you can go out with, people who can help you meet other people
• people with kids, people without kids
• people who like to dress up, people who are ok with casual dress
• people who like fine things, people with everyday tastes
• people with liberal politics, people with conservative views, people who have no views on politics, sports and religion
• people who go to lunch with others, people who bring their own lunch
• people who are talkative, people who are quiet
• people who are just like you or people who are refreshingly different.

## LOCATION/LIFESTYLE - WHAT DO YOU NEED IN A LOCATION TO THRIVE?

*Things you must have :*

*Things you can't stand :*

## PEOPLE - WHAT QUALITIES DO YOU NEED IN THE PEOPLE YOU WORK WITH?

*People you want to be with:*

*People you can't stand :*

*Work Conditions* - What do you need in your work environment to thrive? What would you find intolerable?

Examples:

• corporate culture: clear mission, employee oriented, investor oriented, customer oriented, top down management, flat organizational structure with autonomy for employees

• set own goals, respond to the demands of managers

• stable operating conditions, constant crisis mode

• micro-managing supervisors, co-operative atmosphere, grateful customers, rude customers, no customer contact, frequent client contact

• flexible tasks and assignments, routine tasks, boring assignments, constant challenges, laid back atmosphere, tight deadlines, flexible goals

• frequent travel, constant communications

• working in teams, working alone, work with others, work in isolation

• training opportunities, no need for further training

• individual workspace, new equipment, cramped quarters, tiny cubicles, clean work space, cluttered space, windows, break rooms

• physical amenities, gymnasium, lunch room, catered lunches, ping-pong table

• bicycle lockers and showers, free parking in the city, out in the country

• indoors, outdoors

## WORK CONDITIONS - WHAT DO YOU NEED IN YOUR WORK ENVIRONMENT TO THRIVE?

*Things you must have or would really like :*

*Things you can't stand or don't need :*

6.5

# SETTING YOUR GOALS & PRIORITIES

*Wandering lost in the woods, Alice in Wonderland encountered the Cheshire Cat.*

Alice asked: "Would you tell me, please, which way I ought to go from here?"

The Cat responded: "That depends a good deal on where you want to get to."

Alice said: "I don't much care where ... so long as I get somewhere."

The Cat concluded: "Then it doesn't much matter which way you go. You're sure to (get somewhere), if only you walk long enough."

Someone else once said: *"If you don't know where you're going, you're already there."*

Bob Dylan once said: "... and this ain't no place to be."

*What I say is that if you don't know where you want to go, you're not going to get there. The point is that you have to set goals.*

Right now, your most immediate goal might be to grab a cup of tea. You have to think beyond that. You have to think about tomorrow and the next day, and about next year and the years after that.

When it comes to your career, it is certain that you will be focused on what comes next and what your next move will be. But what is the point of that if it is not connected to some larger context, purpose and direction in life? Perhaps all you want now is to find a survival job, something that will keep you moving along or moving towards the next step. Perhaps you just want something that will get you started on the right path. Even if that is all you want, you need to have some idea about where the path might lead or where you want it to take you. That is what the Cheshire Cat was trying to tell Alice.

Sometimes when people dare to dream about the future and future possibilities, they become paralyzed. It seems so far and so hard and so impossible. Sometimes people are immobilized because nothing seems to be happening now and it is hard to imagine that there might be some life beyond the immediate horizon. Your task now **is to dare to imagine**. Even if you can't get there from here and even if you can't do it today, you need to have the dream in mind.

*A career counseling issue that often comes up with adolescents is that they set their sights on "impossible" goals. A young kid will say that he plans to become an NFL quarterback and that he has no other interests or goals. Those advising him could set him straight. They could tell him that it is an almost impossible goal. My view is that if that's the goal, it should be encouraged. What would I tell that young man? I would say that he needs to stay out of trouble and to work hard and study hard. If you want to be an NFL quarterback, you have to finish high school and get into college and maintain eligibility for the team. You have to exercise regularly and stay away from drugs and alcohol. I would tell him to do all of the things I would tell him to do if he told me that he wanted to be an accountant. I would tell him to have dreams and to set goals and to see where the path might lead.*

*First, you will make a list of your long-term goals.*

What are your long term goals? What would you like to do over the next seven to ten years? Here are some examples: have a well established career, buy a house, get a graduate degree (a Masters or a Ph.D.), get married, have a family, move into management, start a business, develop a consulting practice, travel, write a book... List whatever you dream of doing!

*Second, you will make a list of your short-term goals.*

What are your short term goals? What would you like to accomplish in the next three to five years? Here are some examples: get a job, start your career, get a car that runs, pay off your bills, travel, get your own apartment …

*Finally, make a list of your immediate goals.*

What do you want to accomplish in the next few days, weeks or months, in the next six months or before the year ends? These are more immediate goals and they will be the things you focus on first. They set you up for success in your longer term goals. They will be your to "do list". Here are some examples: build your career binder, clean off your desk, finish writing your resume, start making appointments for informational interviews, buy a new outfit for interviews, finish reading this book, enroll in that class you need, move to another city, start an exercise program, get your car fixed... and so on.

Your short term goals - "To Do" list - should be should be revised on a regular basis.

Keep your longer term goals where you can see them and think about them regularly, and revise them as you move along but at least every six months.

Imagine yourself visiting a foreign city. What do you always have in your pocket, close at hand? You have a map so you don't get lost. These lists are your maps. Keep them handy and keep them up to date.

## 6.6

# PROCRASTINATION WASTES YOUR TIME AND YOUR LIFE

Delay, delay, delay… we all do it. We avoid doing what we should be doing, putting it off until later. Everyone knows someone from the neighborhood who is still sitting on the couch with their parents at age 35. Like in the movie *Failure to Launch*, they just never reach their potential. Procrastination disrupts your ability to be successful.

Procrastinators delay a lot of things thinking that they have unlimited time to recover and do what is important in life - later. Well it doesn't really work that way. There are things that need to happen at different stages of life or they are just not going to happen.

This life has a beginning, a middle, and an end. At each stage there are milestones to be met. As life expectancies have expanded, people often believe they can extend the deadlines for accomplishing things or realizing their full potential. It is not impossible to do what you want later, but it is a whole lot harder if you start from zero at 25, 35, or 40, than if

you have a planful life with accomplishments all along the way.

Procrastination actually takes a whole lot more energy than just doing it. But what should you be doing? That is the big problem. People don't really know what they should be doing at any given time unless they have developed a plan for what they really want in life.

The same thing is true with career actualization. Actualization is a term used in psychology to describe the drive that we each have to do well in life… to reach our full potential. Gaining traction in your career starts early and needs to progress all along the way with the acquisition of experiences that enhance your focus and your employability.

If you want to get somewhere in life it is essential to focus on a goal, that you can develop into a plan, and organize into tasks and activities, that can be accomplished.

***List your goals and set your priorities.*** Every six months make a list of what you want to accomplish. Then set your priorities. You cannot do everything, so go through your list and mark an A next to your highest priority goals. Then assign a number to each "A" goal – A1, A2, A3 etc. Next, run a line through any non-A goals (they will surface on your next 6-month list if they are important enough). Next, take your A1 goal and make a list of the tasks you must complete to make it happen.

***Develop a plan with a timeline.*** Your plan is your dream of how life will be if you take control of your time and your life and decide that you want to move forward on your goals. Once you have outlined your plan, decide how you will accomplish the goal with a timeline of milestones you will meet by certain dates. For example, if getting a professional license is on your list of goals you will need to meet deadlines: register for the exam, register for prep classes, post the exam on your calendar, set up a study group to review the material, join professional organizations, network with professionals in your field, get a career working in an environment that allows you to accumulate qualifying hours, etc.

**Get organized! Make a to do list.** Every day make a list of the things you plan to accomplish. Mark each item with how long it will take (Call Sam - 3 minutes). Then plow through your list. If you are tightly scheduled look for gifts of time where something changes or is canceled. Then make a quick call or send a quick email. Everyone is busy. Work around your busy schedule to find time. Use your time to move your A1 goal forward.

*Schedule your time.* Each and every one of us has 24 hours in a day. Everyone has discretionary time. That is the time you are not sleeping, not in class, studying, or at work — time you control. Use your discretionary time wisely by planning ahead and scheduling important tasks that move your A1 forward.

*Don't waste your time!* Time is ticking on your A goals. There is an "expiration date" timer that is ticking. At every stage in life you have things that must be accomplished... crawling, walking, talking, grammar school, high school, college, internship, career, house, spouse, mouse, promotion, travel...

Once you get your degree it is important to get a job as soon after graduation as possible. Six months is the deadline. It is also critical after job loss that you move back into employment with in six months. If you have not obtained a job after six months, employers are going to wonder what is wrong with you and what have you been doing with your time. Forget about the recession... if you are failing to get a job or develop some other productive use for your time you are going to be damaged by this.

Procrastination is both about failure to plan and wasting time. It is also about laziness. Procrastinators are fooling no one. Procrastinators show up late for everything and they fail to

deliver. And everyone knows it. They think they can get away with it because no one calls them on it. But reality is, everyone notices. Every time you fail to deliver, you are casting an impression of incompetence. Every time you show up late, you are casting an impression of inconsideration.

Excuses, excuses, and more excuses... people tell me they want a change - they hate their job or whine that they don't have a job, but they don't go to job fairs or look for work because they don't have time... Really? With a 24/7 Internet and email you can research companies and jobs, link with professionals on Linkedin, write a resume and get it to employers who are hiring right now. There really are no excuses.

Why do people procrastinate? Procrastinating is a problem for everyone at one time or another. It becomes a serious problem when it keeps you from getting to the important things in life. Disorganization, overbooking, wasting time doing unimportant things, lack of focus, fear of rejection, fear of failure are all part of the problem.

Fix it, get over it, and get on with your life!

07

# PUTTING IT
# ALL TOGETHER

## 7.0

# PUTTING IT ALL TOGETHER: YOUR CAREER CHART

> Career Personality Type
> Motivated Skills Assessment
> Work Values and Priorities
> Key Knowledge Areas
> Life Interests and Passions
> Your Ideal Life/Work Environment
> Your Goals and Priorities

First, let's look at what we've done before moving on to Developing a Career Search Strategy!

When we looked at Career Planning Challenges and the tasks that lie ahead, I said that there were five challenges that you face. We're almost done with the first three:

### ORGANIZATION

Getting organized with a career binder: creating a space for your ideas and inspirations, developing a success timeline, setting up a daily to-do list and calendar and creating a place to keep your contact notes and all of the applications and resumes you will send.

### AWARENESS

Becoming aware of who's hiring and how change happens and affects you, and learning how to research career options.

### FOCUS

Gathering information about yourself through self-assessment.

The last task for the Focus Challenge is pull together all of the information you've obtained from the self-assessments:

*Make sure you've done all of the Self-Assessment exercises before you move to the next step!*

*Now, let's put it all together!* To "put it all together," you are going to create a statement of purpose, using the information you gathered in the previous exercises.

### USE THE CAREER CHART ON P.86-87 TO HELP VISUALIZE YOUR CAREER SEARCH STRATEGY ▶

*Use the information you gathered during the self assessment to complete your summary statement. This is your Statement of Purpose!*

## 7.1

# JOB SEARCH CORRESPONDENCE: *THE ESSENTIAL LETTERS YOU WILL USE TO GET HIRED*

Job related correspondence is often treated like an afterthought, something that should go at the end of the book. In fact, you will be writing to a number of people and for a number of reasons from the start to the end of the job search process.

Many people are intimidated when it comes to sending formal correspondence to potential employers. They know that there is a lot riding on it. *The key is to keep the communication short, clear, and focused.* It is not that difficult if you know what to include and if you edit and review your letter carefully before sending!

Although not necessarily difficult to prepare, these are some of the most challenging letters you will ever write. *We will be looking at some templates or samples you can use.*

Today, in most cases you will be communicating by email. Email has changed everything - the U.S. Mail is just not fast enough for job seeking purposes.

The "thank you" note is still sometimes sent by mail and hand written- not always though- it is a judgment call. It depends on what type of job you are applying for and what type of impression you are trying to make. If it is a counseling job for example, you might want to go soft tech. Think about who you are sending your note to, what job you are applying for and what stage of the process you are in. If it is a software developer job you are probably going high tech.

But everything else happens in a heartbeat these days, and hiring decisions are frequently made in a matter of hours. If you are unable to respond to opportunity instantly, you are out of the loop. You need to be able to send a resume and cover letter quickly. You need to send your thank you letters on the day of your interview.

Keep in mind that you may be sending similar correspondence to different people. It is perfectly fine to recycle your letters, after you have downloaded a template and edited it or adjusted it for the next person or next company. But make sure you check it each and every letter carefully: is the date correct? is it addressed to the right person? does it reference anything specific (job title, company name, industry) that does not apply? Check it line by line before you hit send!

Also, if you are copying text from one document to another, or even sometimes just from one email to another, you may need to run it through a generic text editor first. When you cut or copy from here and from there, unwanted formatting may get thrown in, and it may not show up on your screen. If you paste it into Notepad or Text Editor and then copy it from there, you will be sure to get rid of anything strange.

Sometimes the letter you send will simply be an email. In other cases, you will attach your letters as documents to your email. If you are sending something as an attachment, make certain that you have given a brief description or introduction to the attachments in the email message.

> Always make sure you have given all of your contact information in every email. You don't want someone having to search for it. Design a signature that includes your name, cell number, and your email address. (Do not include any quotes or "happy face" icons below your signature on job related email).

If you decide to attach your letters as documents instead of as an email I would suggest that you use the same header as you use on your resume with your name, address, phone, and email address. In other words the header of your resume is the letter head of all of your letter documents.

*Letters used in job searches include:*

## LETTERS OF INQUIRY
*See sample letters (pp. 74-75)* ▶

Letters of inquiry are perhaps your first foray into contacting an employer. In this letter you are asking the employer or company representative for information or a chance to meet to gain more information about the company and opportunities for individuals with your qualifications.

A computer-engineering student sent a "letter of inquiry" to a local electronics firm, using the contact section of their web site, requesting a meeting to explore opportunities as she was nearing graduation. She had sent a blind email through their web site indicating that she was a student and that she was interested in finding out about the company. A representative from the company immediately responded to her email and invited her to visit and tour the company. At the end of her visit they offered her a job.

## COVER LETTERS
*See sample letters (pp. 76-78)* ▶

Cover letters are sent to employers along with a resume to explain to an employer why they are receiving your resume. The first paragraph tells the employer which position you are applying for and how you learned of their position. The second paragraph tells the employer about your qualifications. The third paragraph tells the employer what the next step will be.

Cover letters must be absolutely perfect in every way. The formatting is typically business letter style or slightly modified if you do not know the name of the individual doing the hiring. Examples in this section show both types of letters.

Any errors in your letter will automatically eliminate you from consideration for any available positions. You will need to have your cover letter as well as your resume proofed by someone who is ruthless with a red pen.

Cover letters are sometimes formatted directly in email or attached as a document along with your resume, in which case your email is a very short introduction to your cover letter and resume.

## THANK YOU LETTERS
*See sample letters (p. 79)* ▶

Thank you letters are one of the best ways to get yourself noticed by an employer. If you are one of the top candidates being considered, you will set yourself apart from the pack by impressing the employer with your thoroughness and thoughtfulness.

Thank you letters are sent immediately after the interview, thanking the employer for the time he/she spent interviewing you. They can also be used to correct a weak answer given in the interview. "I do feel I could have answered the Verilog coding question more effectively. If I had a second chance to answer the question, here is how I would answer it…"

I worked with a young engineering candidate, a number of years ago, who sent a thank you letter to CH2M Hill, even after he had been told he was not going to be hired. He indicated in his letter that he was still interested and found the interview process to have been a great learning experience. When the candidate who was hired didn't work out, he was offered the job!

## RECOMMENDATION LETTERS
*See sample letter (p. 80)* ▶

Recommendation letters are what I call your "walk-on-water" letters. It is a letter that you ask a former employer, a professor, a co-worker, or a co-team member of a project to write for you. The recommendation letter tells the employer that you are an exceptional candidate. You will need to ask someone who you trust will write glowing things about you. (see the section on references)

These letters are written for candidates for graduate school, law school, and the military as well as for job prospects.

You will need to provide the letter writer with

the most important points.

Sometimes the individual writing the letter will ask you to write the letter, highlighting your best qualities relative to the job. That means you must construct the letter for yourself. You will need to identify your best qualities, knowledge, and skills relative to the employer's needs.

## FOLLOW-UP LETTERS
*See sample letters (p. 81)* ▶

A follow-up letter is a letter that you send after an interview, or after an informational interview, or after an offer has been made. This letter is meant to hurry things along but it can't look like you are rushing things. It is your way of showing an employer that you are thoughtful, interested, and following up. It has to capture just the right tone without being pushy. It demonstrates enthusiasm and interest and impresses the hell out of employers! Very few people actually write a follow up letter so it is going to make you stand out from the crowd.

A poorly worded letter can cause irreparable harm so be careful!

## JOB OFFER ACCEPTANCE LETTERS
*See sample letters (p. 82)* ▶

The job acceptance letter is a letter that you send after you have received an offer of employment, accepting the offer. It states that you are excited about the opportunity and look forward to working with the company that is making the offer.

## DEAR JOHN LETTERS
*See sample letter (p. 83)* ▶

"Dear John" are letters that are sent in the event you have accepted a job and you later receive a superior offer that you just cannot pass up. You accepted the first offer in good faith but the later offer is exactly what you want to do. You will need to gracefully back yourself out of the situation without burning any bridges. With new graduates this happens when the market is heated and multiple offers are received. This situation is described in the salary negotiation section of this book in the article titled "Which Offer Should You Take". I created the "Dear John" letter when a young student came to me with the dilemma.

She had accepted an offer from Lockheed Martin and later received an offer from Hewlett Packard that was a better professional and personal move- the HP offer allowed her to stay close to her boyfriend.

## VOLUNTEER LETTERS
*See sample letters (pp. 84-85)* ▶

Volunteer letters are your most desperate letters. Sometimes you find that a company you really want to work for is just not hiring. It could be that the entire economy has slowed down. Or it could be that you do not have enough to offer an employer when there are a ton of more experienced people on the market.

You need experience; you need mental stimulation; you need to be able to interact with other professionals in your field so that you do not lose your technical edge or your knowledge base. You also need the contact with people who might eventually be able to offer you a job or refer you to a colleague in another company that is hiring.

I have coached a number of people through the process of volunteering to work in a company that had not planned to take anyone on. It is a spark of innovative thinking that is a win-win for everyone. The employer gets a new, enthusiastic team member that does not cost them anything and you get experience and exposure to current issues. You are in the epicenter of where you want to be instead of alone in your room mopping.

March 15, 2014

Alta Estad, Senior Technical Writer
MasPar Computer Corporation
749 North Mary Avenue
Sunnyvale, CA 94086

Dear Ms. Elstad,

I am currently a student at CSU, Sacramento majoring in Computer Science. I am looking into the field of technical writing as a career, and I was referred to you by Cici Mattiuzzi. Although I am a sophomore here at CSUS, I would like to get a head start in figuring out which direction I want to go in my career so that I can set goals for myself and work towards them. I have gained quite a bit of information on technical writing and editing from my research, however, I feel that I would gain a much greater perspective by speaking with someone in the field.

I would welcome an opportunity to meet with you, if your schedule permits, to discuss your career path and to have an opportunity to actually see your work environment. I would appreciate any information, insight, or help that you could provide. It would also be much appreciated if you could recommend some classes I should take to work effectively as a technical writer.

Allow me to thank you in advance for your consideration of my request.

Sincerely,

Janella Robinson
janellar@email.com

July 17, 2014

W. L. Bean
Vice President, Power Supply
Washington Water Power Company
Box 3727
Spokane, WA 99220

Dear Mr. Bean,

I am exploring career options with various power companies in the Northwest and would appreciate any information that you could send about career opportunities and the activities of Washington Water Power Company. Specifically, I am interested in positions available for power engineers in the area of transmission, distribution and protection.

In December I will graduate from CSU, Sacramento, with a Bachelor of Science in Electrical Power Engineering (GPA 3.75/4.0). I have experience as an engineering intern with Pacific Gas and Electric Company. In addition, my background includes six years of training and experience as an electrician with the International Brotherhood of Electrical Workers Union.

I would welcome an opportunity to speak with someone in the electrical power area of your company to gain information about typical activities and responsibilities of new college hires.

Sincerely,
James J. Smith
James.smith@email.com

# AARON COX

108 Winder Ave, Rocklin, CA  95678      916) 555-7399      aaron_cox_bsme@email.com

April 23, 2009

Mechanical Designer
Composite Engineering, Inc.

Attn: Composite Engineering, Inc. Human Resources:

Enclosed please find my resume for your consideration. I am interested in pursuing the engineering position that you recently advertised on Monster.com. Specifically, I feel I would be able to contribute to your Mechanical Engineering Design Department with my engineering education and nine years of engineering and design experience.

I am competent at designing, trouble shooting and reverse engineering. In 1998, I received a Pinnacle Award for the design and fabrication of a new innovative tool. I have been in charge of purchasing, installing, and modifying equipment, requiring extensive experience using Solid Works and AutoCAD.

I would welcome an opportunity to become part of the Composite Engineering, Inc. team. I can be reached at (916) 555-7399 or the above email address.

Thank you for your time and consideration.

Sincerely,

Aaron Cox

# CHRIS SOE

1008 S. Disney St.

San Mateo, CA, 94401

(650) 555-8737

February 22, 2010

Human Resources Department
Pacific Gas & Electric
San Jose, CA

Dear Hiring Manager,

I am writing to inquire about the Distribution Planning intern position that is posted on the careers page of the PG&E website. I am interested in applying for this position.

Currently I am a senior in Electrical Engineering at CSU, Sacramento and working towards a Power Engineering Certificate. A list of my completed power related courses is listed on my attached resume.

I have participated in two senior design projects, in addition to numerous class presentations and extracurricular club oriented activities. I have acquired the requisite knowledge and skills necessary to be successful in the internship position through my experience and education including:

- Organization with strict attention to details of data calculations and technically written reports.

- Solid work ethic capable of completing deadlines.

- Cooperative with fellow project members including outside project members.

- Proficiency in written and oral presentation skills.

I am very interested obtaining more information about the position that is available. I can be reached at the above email or phone number.

Thank you for your time and look forward to speaking with you.

Sincerely,

Christopher Soe

# ERIC SPRUNG

8760 Sesame Court, Elk Grove, CA 95624 • (916) 555-1212 • generroh@email.com

January 17th, 2013

Dear Ms. Smith,

I learned about the Electrical Engineer 50170027 position (Job ID: 10951) in Davis, CA on your website, and I am interested in further discussing this exciting opportunity. I feel that my combination of academic excellence, extensive analog and digital design work, and project management experience would allow me to add value to the position and your organization.

During over two years of project work for the California Smart Grid Center I have gained extensive experience in analog and digital design, microcontroller programming, and sensor integration using design and simulation tools including PSPICE, Multisim, ADS, and Matlab. In addition, I have worked extensively with power electronics such as power MOSFETs, BJTs, and buck-boost converters to implement a high-current Lithium-ion battery management system. Throughout these projects I have used excellent verbal and written communication skills to conduct project management and team leadership as well as create professional circuit diagrams and IEEE published documentation.

While attending CSU Sacramento, I have also worked extensively with robotics including advanced simulation of Unmanned Arial Vehicle path planning and collision avoidance optimization to validate an IEEE paper under review. In addition, I have implemented complete hardware systems such as a robotic arm with color detection and a collision avoidance robot with remote control. During my coursework in Microwave Engineering I have also gained understanding and experience with PCB layout in Ultiboard. I am also a member of the Deans Honor List and the Tau Beta Pi honor society, graduating Summa Cum Laude with a GPA of 4.00.

Please find my attached resume with full details of my qualification. I would welcome the opportunity to become a part of the FMC Inc. team. I can be reached at (916) 802-0953 or the above email address. I appreciate your consideration and look forward to discussing the Electrical Engineering opportunity with you.

Sincerely,

Eric Sprung

Dear Mr. Moore,

Thank you again for discussing the available mechanical engineering position with me last Friday. I enjoyed hearing about the responsibilities and opportunities that come along with this position. I also appreciate the time you took from your busy schedule to show me around the facility and answer my questions. I am convinced that I would fit in well as a member of the engineering team and that I would quickly be able to contribute effectively to the Intel manufacturing mission.

Thank you again for allowing me the opportunity to interview with you. As you suggested, I will follow up with you by phone by the end of next week if I do not hear from you before then.

I look forward to speaking with you soon.

Sincerely,
Feysal A Manufengr

---

Dear Mr. Breeser,

Thank you for taking the time to speak with me during your visit to CSU, Sacramento. It was great learning about PPM Technologies. The company's diverse activities in engineering and manufacturing of food processing and packaging equipment are particularly interesting to me. I believe that my experience, leadership, and strong work ethic would be an asset at PPM Technologies.

You had indicated that the person who fills this position would need to be able to juggle multiple tasks. This is a challenge I've faced throughout my career. In my positions with B&H Labeling, Trine Labeling Systems, Systems Engineering & Mfg. and CST/Auto Weigh Company, I managed mechanical design from conceptual beginning through production. This included specifications for purchased components, fabrication and machine drawing detail demands, and structured bill of material requirements for cost accounting. My ability to prioritize and multi-task has made me successful in all of my previous positions.

In addition to my success in customer and sales support, I have been able to communicate effectively with production personnel enabling rapid troubleshooting, problem resolution and significant increases in overall productivity.

Although I will complete my BS in Spring 2009, I can be available immediately to work remotely on machine design projects.

Please do not hesitate to contact me if you have any questions about my qualifications

Sincerely,
Jesse A. Cortez

April 22, 2010

Mr. Bob Alcock
Congressman Bob Filner's Office
504 Cannon House Office Bldg.
Washington D. C. 20515

Dear Mr. Alcock,

I am writing at the request of Kim Carroll, an applicant for a press secretary position with the office of Congressman Bob Filner. Kim worked for me as a student assistant from January 2009 to December 2009 in the Career Services Office of the School of Engineering and Computer Science at California State University, Sacramento.

Kim was an absolute pleasure to work with. She took on much more responsibility than is typical for a student assistant, and could be counted on to take initiative to identify and accomplish a wide range of tasks. She is exceptionally bright and talented. Kim has incredible writing skills and can be relied on to handle complex writing assignments including correspondence, research and analysis of information, report writing and editing of documents.

Kim's communication and organization skills are her greatest strengths. I came to rely on her abilities for the coordination of many activities and programs. The many tasks that Kim assisted me with included the coordination of job fairs and career seminars, initiation of contacts with business and industry representatives that employ our students and graduates, handling correspondence, editing articles, maintaining a job information data base, developing an expansive employer file, and organizing a resource library.

While assisting in my office Kim worked with little or no supervision and did a wonderful job. She was by far the best student assistant that I have ever employed.

I trust you will find my comments helpful as you make your hiring decision. Kim would be a valuable asset for the Congressman's office and it is without hesitation that I highly recommend her.

Sincerely,

Cici Mattiuzzi

Dear Ms. Bisharat,

Thank you once again for meeting with me to discuss my interest in working as an intern for the City of Sacramento this summer. The opportunities that you shared sound great. I believe the experience that I could gain would be very valuable as I pursue my degree in urban planning. As we discussed, the possibility of working for multiple departments or multiple individuals with interesting projects is very appealing to me.

After thinking about it for the past few days I realized that as I prepare for my year in London perhaps it might be desirable to work less than full time. I would like to propose a 30-32 hour per week schedule.

With regard to your question about salary, I searched your web site and found salary information on the City of Sacramento web site as shown below. I would like to aim for the higher end of the range if possible.

Class Title: Graduate Student Trainee
Salary: $16.00 -$20.00 hourly

Thanks again! I look forward to hearing from you.

Sincerely,
Elizabeth Mattiuzzi

---

James March
DPG Group
Intel Corporation

Dear Mr. March,

On March 31st, we spoke on the phone about my acceptance of the offer of employment with your group and we agreed upon a starting date of April 25th. You indicated to me at that time, that this start date would be acceptable and that I would receive a call from HR during the week of April 4th to formalize the arrangement and handle the details. I have not received such a phone call and I am wondering what action I should take at this time.

I would appreciate any counseling or advice you might offer as to how I might best proceed with this matter. I'm very excited about coming to work for the DPG Group and I look forward to your response.

Sincerely,
Mohamed Mahmoud

Dear Ms. Garth,

I am delighted to accept your February 28, 2007, offer of employment as a Software Design Engineer (Entry Level) at Hewlett-Packard in Roseville, California at the monthly salary of <INSERT VALUE>.

I have read and understand the conditions of my employment as outlined in your letter. As requested, I will fax the HP Employment Acceptance Form, including the reference number 111213, to 281-926-7261 before March 9, 2010. I am extremely excited about continuing my employment at Hewlett Packard after graduation in May, and I look forward to many new challenges. Thank you for your confidence and support.

Sincerely,
Todd Carter

---

Dear Mr. Mcabe,

I am writing to accept your offer of employment as a RF engineering intern starting Monday, April 16th. I am very excited by the opportunity that this internship affords me. As we discussed I will be starting part time (20 hours per week) until the end of the semester. At this time I expect to increase my part time hours during the summer although I am uncertain as to exactly how many hours I will work as I complete my MS project and my coursework. I will plan to take a week at the end of the semester to decompress from my studies.

Since our last discussion I spoke with my thesis advisor, Dr. Milicia Markovic and developed a plan for finishing my MS project and graduate with an MS in electrical engineering with a concentration in communications by December 2007. I will be working on the thesis with Dr Markovic 15 hours per week throughout the summer and I plan to finish it by the end of August. The project involves a feed forward design, simulating two tone and CDMA signals. The project fits very well with the work that I will be doing for Jampro and will prepare me for a career in RF design.

Thank you for your confidence in my abilities. I look forward to starting my career with Jampro.

Sincerely,
Victoria Breece

February 10, 2012

Ms. Whitsel
Corporate Assistant
Cal ISO
456 37th St.
Folsome, CA 97611

Dear Ms. Whitesel,

I am writing to let you know that I will be unable to accept the offer of employment that you made to me in April. I was extended an offer for an internship with Cal ISO to start on May 21st, 2012. Although I accepted the offer in good faith, I have since received an outstanding offer that is a dream-come-true.

Since I accepted the Cal ISO internship, I was made an offer to work at Disneyland in a summer engineering internship. It has been a life long goal to work for Disneyland and the offer is an unexpected opportunity.

I recognize that this is very late notice. I applied for the Disney internship in early January and heard nothing. I wish that the offer from Disneyland had come earlier.

Please accept my apology for the inconvenience that this late change in my plans may cause you. I truly appreciate the Cal ISO offer and all of the efforts that you made on my behalf.

Sincerely,

Tyler Bal

John Vue

Intel
8010 Foothills Blvd
Roseville, CA 95678 April 29, 2009

Dear Mr. Vue,

Thank you very much for speaking with me last Thursday and encouraging my interest in volunteering my time at Intel this summer. As you requested this letter is to confirm my interest in volunteering and to define more clearly my specific goals. I would like to pursue a volunteer experience in hardware development engineering. I have attached a copy of my resume outlining my qualifications. In this letter I will define my interests in more detail than expressed in my recent discussion with you.

I am presently a senior majoring in Electronics Engineering scheduled to graduate in December of this year. My interest is in computer system design including all levels of systems from workstations to microprocessor based applications and all levels of development from chip layout, timing, peripherals, breadboarding, and programming through finished product development. I believe a good example of my focus is my Senior Project, which uses an Intel MCS-51 family microcontroller, two HP motion controller chips (HCTL-1000) and infrared sensors to control a mechanical micromouse.

This requires both extensive hardware design and programming. The programming is being done in assembly and C. I would like a position dealing either in this or large scale architecture. I believe this interest would fit nicely in terminal and personal computer design at the Roseville Personal Computer Division or working with the larger systems in the General Systems Lab Division.

I would like to work through the summer, on either a full-time or part-time basis. If Intel is only able to accommodate me with a part-time situation, I would prefer afternoons allowing me to take a morning summer school class. There are several reasons that I am anxious to volunteer my time at Intel. I would like experience in a hardware development lab and I wish to determine if Intel is the company that I want to work for following my graduation. It is important to me to pick the right company. Everything I have read over the past several years indicates that Intel is the best place for my interests.

Thank you again. I look forward to hearing from you. I can be reached at 368-1234.

Sincerely,

Dan Slortan

Dan.Slortan@email.com

Dear Tracy,

Thank you for speaking with me after your presentation to the Sac State ASCE meeting on April 15 was very interested in the project that you described. I also had the opportunity to hear Les Ruben speak in CE 146 for Alumni day. After hearing both of you speak I am really impressed with the work that Bennet Engineering does.

As we discussed I would like to pursue the possibility of a summer CE volunteer position with Bennet Engineering. I believe that the diversity of work that Bennet Engineering does would provide me with an excellent opportunity to gain practical engineering experience. I am highly motivated and feel I would be an asset to your firm with my ability to learn quickly, communicate effectively, and work well as a cooperative team member.

As you requested I am sending my resume via email. I am currently a full time student in the first semester of my junior year carrying 18 units. I am passionate about water resource engineering and I am open to work on any project that may broaden my view of the profession. I served as a leader of the design team for the 2010 ASCE water treatment team, which scored second place for design at the Mid Pac competition. Next year I will be the official captain of the team and look forward to winning first place.

Thank you again for taking the time to review my resume and consider my request to volunteer with Bennet Engineering. I believe it would be a mutually beneficial arrangement.

I look forward to hearing from you.

Sincerely,

Dave Harden

(555)-555-5555

## SPECIAL KNOWLEDGE

*This is my special knowledge:*

## INTERESTS

*These are my interests:*

## SALARY EXPECTATIONS

*These are my salary expectations:*

## GEOGRAPHICAL PREFERENCES

*These are my likes:*

*These are my dislikes:*

# 01
## MOTIVATED SKILL:

# 02
## MOTIVATED SKILL:

## 03

### MOTIVATED SKILL:

### WORK VALUES
*These are my values:*

### LIFE GOALS
*These are my goals:*

## 04

### MOTIVATED SKILL:

### IDEAL PEOPLE ENVIRONMENT
*These are my ideal people to work with:*

### IDEAL WORKING CONDITIONS
*These are my ideal working conditions:*

# JOB-SEARCH STRATEGY

## 8.0

# INTRODUCTION: NETWORKING TO YOUR PERFECT JOB

*The key strategy you are going to employ to find a job is to network and go out and conduct informational interviews.* That is how it works. This is by far the best way to find out about jobs and to get connected to the job you want!

*Yes, you want to look for jobs that are posted or advertised.*

*But you need to know that 80% of the jobs out there are never posted.* Some people call it the "hidden job market." And the fact is that people who go direct and have a conversation with someone are the ones who find the jobs!

*The most important tools you need for finding a job are information and contacts:* You gather information by using published sources. You gather more critical and timely information through informational interviews. You use your network of contacts to find and get connected with people to interview. You get the people you interview to give you more contacts.

*Informational interviewing is a tool used by job seekers to help get inside companies to find out about what really goes on in various fields, and to explore career options and opportunities with the people who really know.*

The people you interview are the ones who really know what jobs are available and what the immediate hiring trends are. They know who you should talk to and where you should look.

The important thing to keep in mind is that if you ask someone if they have a job, they're probably going to say "no." That's the end of the conversation. Their response is usually going to be different if they know that you're just looking for information: you want to learn from them, you're not expecting them to give you anything, all they have to do is share their knowledge and their expertise.

When you ask someone to spend a bit of time speaking with you, they are also more likely to say "yes" and let you in the door if you can say: "this is who told me I should speak with you." It's always easy for someone to blow off a complete stranger. People are usually going to be more helpful when you can tell them who sent you and how you are connected.

Everyone who takes my career planning class is required to interview someone who is doing something related to their career interests. Here is how it worked for one of my students:

The student was an intern at a huge federal agency. For his class assignment, he decided he would just interview his supervisor. That was a contact he already had. His supervisor shared information about his career and all the different assignments he has had over the course of his career. It was exactly the type of information the student needed to think about his own career options, the type of information you can't just get out of a book or off the web. And then, he told the student that his wife was an engineer in a private consulting firm here in Sacramento. He said that he would be happy to connect him with her to explore job opportunities in her firm.

*What my student learned is that this is an amazingly interconnected world.* When you explore your options with one person, you not only learn about their career path but you also get access to their network.

Informational interviewing can also be used prior to an interview to help you understand the position requirements and the company's expectations. When you interview, you won't know the answers you need to give unless you have gathered that information in advance.

*One way to approach a contact is to say: "I will be interviewing for a position with your organization next week and I want to get as much information about the organization as I can before my actual interview."*

*If you are just exploring your options, all you have to do is call someone you know who is employed in your field of choice and ask to speak with them about their career.* If you don't know someone, ask everyone you know, family, friends, people you meet, or your professors for a name of a contact in your field. I have coached a bazillion people through this process. The reality is that "who you know" is what will lead you to a job. *The object of the game is to get information and to make connections.*

*When you call to ask for an appointment, be sure to explain that you are exploring your options and that you are a student, a recent graduate or someone who is thinking about making a career change.*

*Next, tell them who referred you, and that you just want a 20 minute appointment.* Be sure to meet with them on site, not on the phone. You will get so much more information and you will forge a much tighter relationship for future hiring possibilities.

*People are impressed when someone takes the time to come in and ask questions.* There are dozens of questions you may want answered, but think about them carefully before you arrive at your interview.

Write your questions down just in case you get nervous, but try not to act like you are interrogating the person. Even though you will have a list of questions, you want to let the conversation flow. You don't want it to appear like you are a rigid survey taker with a preset script. Be sensitive to the time constraints of the person you are talking with and remember

you asked for just 20 minutes.

*The main questions you want to ask your contact is what they do, what is required to be successful in the field, and what advice they would give to someone considering a career in their field or a job with their company.* If you decide that you are interested in their organization, be sure to ask about the best way to get in. You also want to ask if they can recommend other people for you to talk with to gather more information.

Never stop informational interviewing. Find as many people as you can to talk to. Do it formally, do it informally... You will find that it either gets you to a better place or helps you realize you are already where you want to be!

*And remember, this is definitely a situation in which you will want to send a thank you note later!*

## 8.1

# RESEARCHING CAREER & JOB OPTIONS

**Before you go out and try to schedule any informational interviews, you need to identify the industries you are going to focus on and develop a list of companies where you might find opportunities.** And before you contact anyone, you will need to do some research on the companies and industries you're going to be trying to reach.

We have already talked about using published sources of information to conduct research. We went over this before so you could start getting some ideas about the world-of-work and the range of opportunities. You are going to need to keep doing this again, this time focusing on specific companies and specific jobs.

Your Career Chart is your guide for finding the types of companies you want to reach. *As you do research on those companies and the jobs available, you may need to go back and revise your Career Chart. You might also need to revise your Career Chart after you conduct informational interviews and gather information.*

Find Career chart on pp.

*Make sure you do your research before you actually go visit anyone.* Yes, you are going to be doing informational interviews in order to gather information, but your questions will seem smarter and you will seem better prepared to take on a job in the field you are targeting if you already know a fair amount. You don't want someone you interview to think that you are someone who needs to start at square one!

## 8.2

# WHAT YOU WILL LEARN FROM AN INFORMATIONAL INTERVIEW

**The informational interview is not a job interview!** You are not asking for a job and you are not expecting to be offered one. All you are doing is meeting with a professional in your field in an informal way and asking questions about his or her work.

If they think you are there actually looking for a job or expecting one, they are probably not going to meet with you. At this point, they have no reason to offer you an opportunity, they don't know anything about you and you are hardly going to get to meet with anyone if you are only meeting with people who

actually have jobs available.

*I have already told you that the main questions you want to ask your contact is what they do, what is required to be successful in the field, and what advice they would give to someone considering a career in their field or a job with their company.*

---

**This is the information you are trying to gather:**

• information about your career field and about specific jobs
• details about a typical day in your field of interest
• more information about the skills necessary to be successful in a specific career
• the future prospects of a field
• how you fit in with your current level of education and experience
  *You also want to:*
• make contacts for possible job leads and interviews
• develop leads on positions as they become available

---

If you decide that you are interested in their organization, be sure to ask about the best way to get in. You also want to ask if they can recommend other people for you to talk with to gather more information.

The information you gain from these interviews is like gold! People who are working in your field will be able to tell you things you just can't find in any published resource.

It is also the case that if they have taken the time to speak with you, they are going to want to be helpful. They are going to want to feel like it was worth their time. They will want to know that they have helped contribute to the success of someone else.

## 8.3

# HOW TO FIND PEOPLE TO INTERVIEW

*Tell everyone you come in contact with what you are doing- that you are exploring your options and researching the possibilities.*

Remember - it's both what you know and who you know. As you firm up your career focus, talk to people: Talk casually with people whenever and wherever you can. *Be sure to explain clearly what you are interested in.* I have heard of people getting leads in the strangest places like: hot tubs, riding buses, at Greek food festivals, playing volleyball, and from family members at holiday dinners just by sharing their career interests. *"I am exploring careers in financial planning."* After you get a name, call and say: "I got your name from so and so, and I am exploring my options and so and so said you would be a good person to talk to."

One candidate I worked with was on a golf course waiting with a friend to be paired up with another twosome. (Evidently you have to be a foursome to golf...) He and his friend were paired up with a manager from Chevron who by the end of the golf game offered him a job! *Everyone always asks "what do you do?" You need to be prepared with a great answer:* "I am changing careers (or I have recently graduated) and I am researching careers in finance (or urban planning or whatever you determine the keywords that trigger a good response are)."

*Ask people you know:* Ask your contacts such as former professors, career coaches, friends, and relatives for the names of anyone they know who is in a company you are interested in or who is in a field you are pursuing. If they don't know any names of people, ask for the names of companies that are engaged in a specific activity that interests you.

*Local newspapers:* The local newspapers will frequently have published lists of local companies in various industries. *The Business Journal* publishes in markets across the country and your subscription includes the most fabulous books of lists and industry supplements for the markets where they publish. They have lists with company data for every industry from engineering firms and construction firms to hospitals, consulting firms, accounting firms, manufacturers, colleges and universities, private schools, software companies, high tech manufacturers, and everything in between. *This is the best source of company lists across the US that I have ever found!*

*Local university career center:* Talk with the staff at the local university career center about companies that hire in your specific field of interest. They can give you lists and tons of information about companies. Some even post the information on their web sites. This angle might take some resourcefulness on your part, as many university career centers are only open to their alumni and students. I am a big believer in openness and transparency, so at CSUS I keep all of my stuff visible on the College of Engineering and Computer Science site.

*Contact professional associations for information and contacts.* Join associations associated with your profession and attend conventions for leads and information. You will also find job listings and recruiting ads in professional journals. You will also gain valuable information on trends in your field. What is hot and what is not. Most professional associations have web sites and send monthly journals with fabulous articles and jobs listings for their members.

*Alumni club publications:* Use your alumni publication, club, or network to obtain names of individuals who graduated from the same school you graduated from with a similar area of study or career field of interest from whom you might gain information and leads. Who knows, them might be hiring. Who better to know the quality of your background and education?

*Periodicals and Resource Books:* Scan written material such as technical journals, newspapers, magazines, directories for articles on your area of interest, for company names or names of individuals doing things of interest.

*Reference Librarians:* Ask your local reference librarian for any other reference sources for local companies in your area of interest.

*If all else fails, walk into the target company, approach the secretary or receptionist and ask him/her to recommend someone with whom to speak.* Make sure to explain that you are only seeking information, (not a job), about this career. A random entry in the company "contact us" link has also yielded great results. This method has worked quite well for some people.

*Whatever you do, go out there and find people to interview!*

## 8.4

# HOW TO ARRANGE AN INFORMATIONAL INTERVIEW

*How to arrange an Informational Interview:*
01. Telephone the person you are interested in talking with and request a meeting.
02. Explain that you are exploring your career options.
03. Tell them who referred you to them and explain that you really are just seeking advice.

*You absolutely must follow up this phone call with an email* confirming your appointment and indicating how much you are looking forward to meeting with them.

*Always tell the person that you are seeking to meet with that you need only 20 minutes of his or her time* to meet at his or her convenience. Most people - even the busiest - have 20 minutes to share with a person exploring a career field. (Your appointment may last longer, so don't book yourself too tightly.)

*Remember these important rules:*

If you call or write, *be absolutely clear in how you present your request.* You must avoid allowing the person you wish to see, the receptionist or the secretary to assume that you are seeking a job interview. Some individuals have had luck just dropping in and requesting to meet with an individual in a particular department. This is a little dicier than making an appointment.

*Don't be late. Get there on time.* The person you are seeing is doing you a favor. Be businesslike and dress professionally. You don't want to dress like you are there for a job interview, but you want to look nice.

*Don't bring a resume!!!* You can send one after your informational interview, tailored to the needs of the company, if it seems appropriate.

*Prepare your questions beforehand* and write them down to take with you. Ask yourself what you need to know about the occupation, firm or industry. Do your homework!!!

*Dress nicely* but not like you are being interviewed. You want to look business casual rather than like you are dressed in a suit for an interview.

# INSTRUCTIONS FOR YOUR INFORMATIONAL INTERVIEW

―――――

01. Using your contacts from career day, friends, family, faculty, or by making a cold call, contact someone who is doing something that you would like to do or a company you would like to work for. You might even call someone who is mentioned in an article.

02. Write a short introduction as to why you are calling to use while you are begging for a short meeting, just in case you get nervous after you make the call.

Call and schedule an appointment to meet in person. Ask for 20 minutes, but plan that it will take as much as 1 to 2 hours.

Ask open-ended questions.

Be sure to get other names of individuals you might contact before leaving your informational interview. You will want to talk to lots of people in your field to see all the different places that employ people in your chosen field. To get a job you are going to need to network your way into as many companies as you can. So getting the names of other people at the company of the person you are talking to and names of other individuals at other companies will help you move from company to company or from division to division within a company.

Write notes on the results of your Information Gathering visit.

*Send a thank you note! Tell them what you are doing to follow up on the advice they gave you.*

# HOW TO START YOUR INFORMATIONAL INTERVIEW
## & QUESTIONS YOU CAN ASK:

01. Start your interview with a brief statement reminding the person you are talking with why you are there, who referred you, and what you hope to gain. Example: "I am interested in exploring careers in the _____ field. I am trying to get a better understanding of what a person does in this field and what it takes to be successful in this field and how to get into the field. I was referred by so and so who said you'd be a good person to talk with."

What do you do? - Your job title? Ask for a business card at this point.

How did you get involved in this field?

What is your background?

What other types of backgrounds do people in this field have?

What kinds of projects or activities do you work on?

What types of skills are needed for this field?

What makes someone successful in this field?

What is a typical day like?

What do you like best about your job?

What do you like least about your job?

What areas in the field are growing?

How is the future of the field changing?

How is this field tied to economy?

How is it being affected by the current economic climate?

What are the entry-level jobs in this field?

What is the salary range for entry-level jobs? Top-level?

Is there much upward opportunity or room for career growth?

Can you recommend any sources of information for this field - professional associations, publications, or conferences? Who are the other key players in this industry?

Are there any drawbacks to a career in this field or in this industry?

Can you give me the names of any other people that I might speak with for more information?

# HOW TO APPROACH AN INFORMATIONAL INTER-VIEW & QUESTIONS TO ASK

*The basic approach to an informational interview:*

You are in the process of making some decisions about your career, and you want to learn more about the opportunities in a given field for someone with your skills and experience. There is a lot at stake in terms of your future, so you want the best information you can get.

Be prepared for a response such as: "I think our human resources people can probably answer your questions."

You may want to respond with: "I'm sure that would be true if I were looking for a job, but I'd like to talk with you because _____ told me you could give me the best advice and suggested that I would benefit from your experience and insight."

There are dozens of questions you may want answered, so think about them carefully before you arrive at your interview. Write your questions down just in case you get nervous, but don't get too rigid or just read them off. Be sensitive to the time constraints of the person you are talking with and remember you asked for 20 minutes.

*Remember, this should seem like a conversation and not an interrogation.*

**The key to this whole process is enthusiasm.** If you are truly interested in a topic, that will shine through. When it does, the person you are talking with will most likely respond positively.

# AFTER THE INFORMATIONAL INTERVIEW: TASKS AND FOLLOW-UP

*Immediately after the interview, document the contact and place the information in your career binder.* Here's the template I showed you when we were talking about your career binder.

Remember what I said before: even if you keep your contact information in a database, you still need to have this information in hard-copy where you have a place where you can quickly take notes. You need to keep everything organized for easy access and review!

Staple the person's business card to the form, and make sure you have written down the names of everyone they referred you to.

*Next, "debrief" yourself.* You can do this on the contact form. Make sure you have answered the following questions:

• What did I learn?

• How does what I learned fit with my skills, values and interests?

• What else do I need to know? Who else do I need to talk with?

Then, before the day is out, *send a Thank you note.* It only needs to be a few lines long. Express your appreciation and tell them what you plan to do next.

*Finally, review the notes you've taken:* Are there any other action steps to be taken on the basis of the information you obtained?

At the end of each interview, it is time to make certain that you have your next informational interview set up. A really good interview is one that has provided you with names of more people to speak with.

The really best interview is one where you learn that you have found an approachable organization, one that has job opportunities that you can start considering and following up on.

## 8.7

## THE BIGGEST MISTAKES JOB SEEKERS MAKE - FEAR OF APPLYING

The more of these interviews you do, the more likely it is that you will find a company you want to work for and it will be time to start tailoring your presentation (i.e., your resume) to secure that position.

The biggest mistake that unemployed people make is that they hang around with other unemployed people. The second biggest mistake is that they keep their status a secret. It is embarrassing to be unemployed. It is hard to surround yourself with employed people if you spend your day glued to a television set or a computer screen. You will never hear about good job opportunities if you are isolating yourself. If you want to get a job, you need to get out there and meet people and apply! Yes, you will face rejection, but the alternative is just too ugly to contemplate, and furthermore, you don't qualify to be permanently unemployed... Do you?

Places where you will meet people include: job fairs, professional activities and conferences, and by taking specialized training and classes, even if you have graduated. You will be meeting people and enhancing your chances of finding really great opportunities, as well as improving yourself. You might also meet people in casual situations like at Starbucks, on a soccer field, on a golf course, in a hot tub, on a bus, on light rail, or in a bookstore. Over the years, people have told me that they have made valuable and productive contacts in all of these situations. I have heard about people getting jobs or job leads in some of the most unusual places, but I have never heard of anyone getting a job sitting in a closet.

The reality is that if you want a job you have to put yourself out there! 80% of the jobs that are available at any given time are not posted anywhere. That means that you will need to develop a little 1 minute speech where you will describe yourself, telling people what you are interested in. I know you are shy and you are busy and you have a million excuses for not doing the things that I am telling you to do. Do it anyway!

I have been told by many job seekers that it is helpful when I gave them explicit instructions on what to say when calling an employer. So here it is, explicit instructions on what to say when you meet someone at a conference or in line at Starbucks: "Hi my name is (fill in the blank) and I will graduate with a (BA or BS, or whatever) in (Urban Planning, Marketing, Psychology, Computer Science, Engineering or whatever) ... I am studying (fill in the blank) and I am exploring opportunities in (fill in the blank)".

*Scenario 1,* At that point they will jump all over you with "well, we are looking for good candidates in your field". *Scenario 2,* you will start asking questions like: What do you do? What is a typical day? What do you like best about your job? What qualities are required for success in this field/company?

This is not brain surgery. You are trying to make contact and get enough information to figure out where to go with your life. So get out there and just do it! Connect with people. You are not doing yourself any good by sitting on the sidelines with other unemployed people or in the closet hiding.

8.8

# GET MOVING! JOB SEARCH QUICK ORGANIZATION PLAN

*Getting a job is a full time job that requires drive, discipline, and determination.* This is true no matter what your life situation. During the recession so many people were unemployed- it was easy to believe that there were no jobs. Many people just stopped looking, discouraged by the prospects, and discouraged by the process. The news is rife with stories of the long-term unemployed - people who failed to ignite at graduation or whose job flamed out with a layoff notice.

It is easy to just chuck it all and give up looking, give up trying. Even with the recession long over I run into people who believe there are no jobs or that they are too inexperienced or have been unemployed too long to be considered.

*Here is the risk - if you believe there are no jobs or you lack necessary years of experience you will act accordingly.* If you do not look, you will not find a job. If you lack confidence you will sabotage your efforts. Even in the tightest market people get jobs and in great markets employers dig deeper into the pool to find enthusiastic candidates who lack experience; you want to be one of them.

*When things feel hopeless that is the time to buck up and have a plan* - to create your own purpose and your own schedule. It should be an ambitious schedule with time spent on all aspects of self-improvement and self-determination. *YOU DETERMINE WHAT YOUR PURPOSE IS.* At any given time you can make the decision to find your purpose in life. It may not be the one you planned for a few years ago or even a few months ago; but it will be a good one if you commit yourself. Find your greatest strengths and interests. Believe in yourself!

*Get out of bed early.* Sounds simple. But even simple things are difficult when you find yourself without purpose and depressed by the prospects. Depression is a very common affliction of job seekers. One of the best cures is to get moving early. Tumble out of bed at 6:00 am with a plan and a whole world of possibilities will occur to you. You will be taking control of your life once again.

*Start your day with exercise* - running, walking, biking, tennis - all things you can do on the cheap to improve your outlook and your outward appearance. Do it first thing in the morning to get the endorphin kick and clear your head. Put exercise on the schedule just like you would any other appointment. Set the alert on your phone to remind and reinforce your plan. Exercising will open your mind to the possibilities and reduce the stress and anxiety you feel about not having a job. You will start to think about what you should be doing to move on with your life.

Exercise with a partner and you have your morning office meeting right there on the trail - and you will have the support you need for your new beginning. The support and encouragement will help tremendously. Bounce your ideas as you bounce your body!

*Carve out a space where you can work each day.* It is amazing how just having a place to go will make you more productive. A corner of a room or Starbucks works — as long as it is a place you feel comfortable and motivated to produce.

*Set your goals.* Start this process by listing your long-term and your short-term goals. What do you want to accomplish over the next 3 to 6 months? What do you want to accomplish over the next 3 to 5 years? Write a "to do" list each day with your goals in mind.

*Get organized!* Put together a job search binder and a calendar to organize your search. Your job search is an adventure... an opportunity to explore your field, meet new people, and find openings. Be positive – people will respond accordingly.

*Get help!* Doing it alone is arduous at best – find a career counselor, or a career planning class (or read a career-planning book!). You need to establish a solid strategy for getting a job and this is where to start. A professional can help move the process along with better results. (You would not try to set your own broken leg would you?)

*Be well informed.* Read the news for the geographical area you are searching for a job in and search professional journals for exciting breakthroughs, professional activities, ideas, and leads. Develop a list of possible companies to apply with and hit their web sites. Research a minimum of ten companies on your target list each day. You will be amazed how many companies are actually hiring. You only need to find one job – right?

*Network!* Use your contacts to connect with people inside of the organizations that interest you. Linkedin or friends and faculty can provide you with names of persons you might connect with for more information or a company visit. Send email expressing interest in the organization and describing your qualifications. Follow up with telephone calls and schedule appointments.

*Follow-up* with thank you email to anyone and everyone who gives you ideas, contacts, or leads. And get used to some rejection... don't let it stop you! Just get more creative the next time.

*People are getting hired now – Do not give up!*

## 8.9

# SUCCESSFUL CAREER AND JOB OPTION RESEARCH EXPERIENCE

Most people will do anything to avoid or postpone their job search. While helping my daughter on her quest to find a summer internship it became quite obvious to me how difficult people find job seeking because it requires talking to people. Many people engage in the most unproductive activities, ones that require the least direct contact with people. Monster.com is a great avoidance tool. All you have to do is paste your resume into place and then go back to whatever else you would rather be doing. But the reality is that you have to talk to people to get a job.

My daughter was in town for a week for spring break of her freshman year in college trying to find a summer internship. She sent her resume out a couple of months before to a number of organizations expecting that when the summer arrived someone will just call her and offer her the perfect position. When I told her she needed to follow up she was perplexed. "Why don't they just hire me because I am good? Can't they see that from my resume?" She complained. To which I responded "because they don't know you are good unless they meet you and see that you can walk and chew gum at the same time."

I instructed her to network with people to get leads and introductions to people who were well connected in the Capitol and at the California EPA. These were the places she wanted to intern. I responded to her anxiety over making calls: It will most likely be a person that you have met that will hire you. I told her "This is an interconnected society. Making contacts will lead you to the perfect job. People help each other. That is why the contacts you make are important. You have to cultivate and nurture contacts not for what you can get but because that is what community is: it is helping each other get through life. Think of it as having a cup of tea with people... keeping in touch with people, keeping up with people's lives". Email makes it even easier to make contact and connect in a big world.

So after a little bit of prodding she sent emails, made several phone calls, and set up appointments for the week. We practiced her approach from the handshake (with eye contact and a smile), to giving her name and explaining that she was there to explore the possibility of a summer internship. As we went through the routine, I noticed little tears streaming down her face. I asked her why she was crying and she said, "I am afraid". I guess we are all afraid of rejection. I said, "These are nice people and are going to be nice to you. Even the people you will meet for the *first time will be nice."* We assembled a great outfit and off she went on Monday morning to meet with people. She came home absolutely gushing with how nice people were to her, both on the phone and in person. She had a very encouraging phone call with a person at the Air Resources Board who sent her resume around and had several promising "bites." She had a fantastic tour of the Capitol with a family friend, and interviewed in an assembly woman's office and scheduled more appointments. The day after her meetings she sent thank you notes to everyone. She finally "got it"! (And she also got a great internship with the California Air Resources Board!)

As a postscript - the people who she did her internships with during her undergraduate summers are the people who wrote her stellar letters of recommendations that got her into graduate school. Internships and summer jobs during college are some of your most valuable experiences. They help you launch your future in so many ways. They provide you with a network of people who nurture you, teach you the ropes, and who promote your career.

## 8.10

# NETWORKING TO YOUR PERFECT JOB IS A CONTACT SPORT!

The vast majority of people who attend job fairs are uncertain about what to do next. They connected with interesting possibilities, but they are at a loss about how to close the deal.

***Job seeking is a contact sport.*** You have to interact with people to get hired. It is not easy for the timid. It is not something that comes natural. No one really tells you how to do it when you are growing up. Job seeking for the first time is like jumping off of a cliff... You have to throw yourself out there.

***Most jobs are never posted***. Jobs do not just fall into your lap. The fact is that people who go direct and connect with people are the ones who find the jobs! You have to get out there and meet people who have the power to hire you or the people who can connect you to them.

Whether you were intimidated or totally at ease with meeting potential employers, after a job fair you need to take it to the next level. You have ***to*** take the leap... If you found an interesting company, you have to go beyond the job fair to an on site visit and then you have to turn it into a job offer. You need to learn as much as you can about a potential employer and work environment to see if it is a good fit. The only way to do that is to actually visit.

*Ask for a second date – Information Gathering.* Connecting directly with people by informational interviewing gets you inside companies to see what really goes on and to explore career options and opportunities with the people who really know – people who are doing what you want to do! This is by far the best way to find out about jobs and to get connected to the job you want! They are also the ones who really know what jobs are available and what the immediate hiring needs and trends are. And they know who you should talk to next.

***Connections are important for success in Information Gathering.*** It is easy for someone to blow off a complete stranger. People are usually going to be more helpful when you can tell them who sent you and how you are connected.

When you call to ask for an appointment, be sure to explain that you are exploring your options and that you are a student, a recent graduate or someone who is thinking about making a career change.

Be sure to meet with them on site, not on the phone. You will get so much more information and you will forge a much tighter relationship for future hiring possibilities.

People are impressed when someone takes the time to come in and ask questions. There are dozens of questions you may want answered, but think about them carefully before you arrive at your interview. Be sensitive to the time constraints of the person you are talking with and remember you asked for just 20 minutes.

The main questions you want to ask your contact is what they do, what is required to be successful in the field, and what advice they would give to someone considering a career in their field or a job with their company. If you decide that you are interested in their organization, be sure to ask about the best way to get in. You also want to ask if they can recommend other people for you to talk with to gather more information.

## 8.11

# MONSTER.COM: A MONSTER WASTE OF TIME

The odds are that you are not going to find a job by searching Monster or posting a resume there. In fact, no one actually knows what your chances are. Monster cannot and certainly will not tell you. What is known is that when you look at the available numbers, Monster looks more like a canary than an 800 pound gorilla.

The data are hard to come by because there is really no way to accurately track how people have come to find their jobs. The question is also complicated by the fact that you can look at this from the perspective of an employer (are they finding the candidates they need?) and from the perspective of the job seeker (are they getting jobs?). The number of struggling job seekers can only be known from the unemployment data. A further complication arises because there is no real measurement available distinguishing between entry level job seekers and lower skilled workers on one hand, and advanced career professionals and highly skilled workers on the other hand.

### DOES MONSTER.COM WORK?

One analysis I read tried to tackle this question by comparing the number of new jobs that are created each month to the number of people who are newly hired each month, as reported by the U.S. Department of Labor. If every single job available were to be listed at Monster (or on other job boards), the theoretical maximum would be that you have a 7 percent chance of getting a job through Monster or some other online job board. But job boards are not the primary source of new hires, and if you conservatively estimate that 50% of new hires come from other sources (which I will discuss below), then the theoretical maximum chance you would ever have for finding a job through Monster drops to 3.5%.

Another analysis I read approached the question by looking at the number of resumes posted at Monster relative to the number of jobs posted. The ratio of jobs to resumes is about 3%.

A survey done in 2000 (yes, it's old but it was during the dot-com hiring boom and pre-9/11) asked successful job seekers how they found their positions (Forrester Research). Only 4% said that they found their jobs by using the internet (that is the whole web, not just Monster). This is the same estimate that career guru Richard Bolles gives based on his observations.

Another survey that has been conducted yearly since 2002 (by CareerXroads) asked employers (90% of whom used Monster) how they found their new hires. In the first go around, Monster was credited as the source of about 1.5% of hires. That figure has improved and now stands somewhere in the 3 to 4% range.

With respect to my perspective, I can only provide you with anecdotal data. I know a lot of job seekers who have signed up at Monster and devoted time to it. The number of success stories I can recount is way below 3% and actually much closer to zero.

Instead of hearing success stories, I have heard about people inundated with email advertisements, about jobs that are really work-at-home scams, about jobs that are filled or do not seem to exist and about pitches made by recruitment firms that are seeking a supply of heads to use as a tool to sell their services to companies with actual jobs.

## HOW DOES MONSTER WORK?

First, let me say that it is not just Monster and CareerBuilder. There are dozens of career opportunity sites on the web. The business model is fairly simple. They sign up thousands or millions of job seekers and keep them coming back with advice and services of all kinds. Because they can claim access to hordes and hordes of job seekers, they can charge HR (human resources) professionals large sums of money to post their jobs. And then they can sell the HR people access to the resumes of prospective employees. And at the same time, they can sell premium services to the job seekers.

The business model does not require it to be a good source of new hires or a good way to find a job. All it requires is the ability to generate traffic and to sell the numbers to those on both sides of the hiring equation. The business model depends on traffic and perception, not success.

The same model applies for the job recruitment shops that shop for heads through Monster. There was one recently featured in TIME magazine that focuses on "moms." When the story for TIME was written, the "Mom Corps" had almost 650 job seeking moms for every job they had listed. If you do the math on the numbers they gave for their success since in placing applicants since their 2005 founding, it looks like every applicant has less than 1% chance of getting a job through them.

## HOW DO PEOPLE ACTUALLY FIND JOBS?

I referred above to the CareerXroads annual survey - a large scale survey of employers. What they found is that about 35% of jobs are filled from within the company. With respect to external hires, the companies surveyed said that at least 30% of jobs are filled by referrals (i.e., people using their contacts). About 20% of the newly hired found the job through the company website. About 8% of new hires come from "direct sourcing," which basically means corporate recruiting. College recruiting, career fairs and open houses, print advertising, outside recruitment agencies, and contract-to-hire (or temp-to-hire) each account for about 3% of jobs filled. "Other" sources account for about 10%. And finally, internet advertising accounts for about 12%.

If you add up the numbers, you will find that there is not much room left for Monster or any other career opportunity site to dominate the hiring market. Monster and the other career sites tend to account for the amount of hires that can be expected: somewhere around 3% to 4%.

## WHY DOES MONSTER PERSIST?

HR personnel have a lot of money to spend on recruiting, and they spend close to half of it on online advertisements. To them, it seems to make sense. Millions of people are searching online, so it can seem like a good way to find employees.

But there is another person in the equation: the hiring manager. In other words, the HR department may be responsible for finding new employees, but it is the hiring manager who will decide who gets the job.

Hiring managers say that better than 60% of the people they find come from "word of mouth referrals" (Forrester Research).

On the other side of the equation, the desperate job seeker is looking for any crumb that is thrown their way.

There is also a big unknown factor at work here.

As I mentioned above, there is a big difference between a twenty year career veteran with tons of experience and a student graduating from college. There is also a difference between a highly trained and specifically skilled job seeker and one who is looking for work on the basis of more basic and general work aptitudes. If you have highly specialized skills, perhaps someone will contact you in response to your posted resume. A number of job seekers in the fields of engineering, computer programming and information technology have told me that they have had some measure of success in getting interviews by posting at Dice.com. But if your skill set is similar to ten thousand other people competing for one particular job, there is no reason to expect that your name will be the one that is picked out of the fish bowl to win the prize.

When we look at the modest success rate for those who do find work through Monster, what we don't know is how many were part of that highly skilled and highly sought after group, and how many were just a face in the crowd.

So what is the takeaway message here?

First, the age old wisdom about job seeking still applies: you need to use your contacts and you need to make new contacts through informational interviewing. Your best bet is that someone will give you the name of someone who knows someone who can tell you about an opportunity.

Second, the want ads are a time honored vehicle for finding employment. Yes, you need to look at the want ads, both online and in the newspaper, and in professional journals. But you do not want to make this your only method and you do not want to spend inordinate amounts of time on this. As you know, you can spend huge amounts of time searching through Monster and other sites and applying for jobs. If the yield is predictably low, that is not where you want to invest your time and energy.

Third, I have no reason to believe that it is useful to post your resume at Monster or any other such site. And there is reason to suggest that you should not. I mentioned above that what I repeatedly hear is that after posting a resume, people end up wasting tons of time on bogus offers and email spam.

And there's a risk involved. On January 23rd, 2009 (and for months thereafter), Monster had the following message posted at their website:

*"We recently learned our database was illegally accessed and certain contact and account data were taken, including Monster user IDs and passwords, email addresses, names, phone numbers, and some basic demographic data. The information accessed does not include resumes. Monster does not generally collect — and the accessed information does not include - sensitive data such as social security numbers or personal financial data."*

Isn't that great? The thieves did not get your social security number.

## HERE IS MY ADVICE:

———

Yes, keep your eye on posted job announcements. I have been impressed with Indeed.com as a search tool for this purpose. Indeed.com aggregates job announcements from a number of sources, including Monster and Careerbuilder. Instead of hopping from one job board to the next, let the search engine provide you all of that information in one place.

And you can also just use Google search. Google picks up everything in Indeed.com and everything from corporate and government websites.

Searching the web for job opportunities is actually an important part of the career research process. Even if it is not how you are going to find a job, it is an important task relative to understanding your options and understanding the employment playing field.

Bottom line: Yes, you should surf the web for job opportunities. Just make sure you are not wasting time.

09

# RESUMES & PORTFOLIOS

## 9.0

# PRESENTING YOURSELF WITH A RESUME: RESUMES EXPLAINED

*So how do you convey to an employer that you are the perfect candidate?* If you are going to get the attention of an employer and get the job, you need to stand out from the crowd. *You have five ways of showing employers that you have the right stuff:* your cover letter, your resume, your portfolio, your interview and last but not least, your enthusiasm.

You need to have an extremely well designed resume that makes it clear that you are the perfect candidate. An employer will look closely at your resume to find courses, project experience and work experience that fit with their needs. They will also want to know that you have a certain combination of soft skills that will allow you to perform well on the job. There are three areas of your life that you can mine for the knowledge and skills that employers want: your education, your experience and your extracurricular activities. If you have not already completed all of the SELF ASSESSMENT EXERCISES, you need to do that now, before you start working on your resume. That is where you have cataloged the most important information that will appear on your resume.

To begin with, employers want to hire candidates who can demonstrate that they have the technical expertise that fit with the job requirements. Your degree from an accredited university goes a long way in telling the employer that you have the right stuff. Show your degree(s), certification, your courses, and describe any projects you have that are relevant to the needs of an employer. Your course list and class projects will show that you have learned things that make you likely to succeed in a particular position. The project experience you have had, either in a career related internship or job, also shows that you have the technical expertise you need to perform on the job. In the real world, projects are the primary focus of a technical professional. Show your projects prominently!

Employers will also assess whether you have basic soft skills that give you the ability to perform well in their work environment. Being a good student is not enough to get you a job. You will need to demonstrate to an employer that you have successfully used your soft skills too. Potential employers want to know that have you have learned how to manage a project, lead teams, worked as an effective member of a team, worked with customers effectively, as well as how to stand up and give a great Power-Point presentation. Be sure to share it all.

Your cover letter, resume, portfolio and actual interview should all convey the same message and work in concert to show the employer you have what they need. You may feel you are repeating yourself, but actually you are reinforcing the message over and over again. When you get to the interview, your resume and the work you put into it will help you stay on message and avoid rambling, and it helps the employer grasp your true strengths.

Lastly, enthusiasm for what the employer does also goes a long way to making you a fabulous candidate. Chase what you love and ignore the rest. Being the perfect candidate means chasing the right job.

## RESUMES EXPLAINED

Your resume is probably your most important job-seeking tool. It is frequently the thing that gets you noticed first. Writing an effective resume is one of them most tricky parts of your job search.

It really needs to be well thought out and focused on the industry and the employers you are targeting.

Before you write a resume it is essential to know what you want to do, and who you are relative to employers' needs. To develop a good understanding of what you need to convey in your resume it is helpful to analyze the job description for the types of positions you are pursuing. It is also important to speak with people in your chosen field (this is why we focused on informational interviewing). Ask them what they look for in a candidate and what qualities are necessary to be successful.

Before you start trying to write your resume, it is helpful to have a job description to help you focus. A good place to find great job descriptions is the Occupational Outlook Handbook (OOH). The wording you will find for various occupations is incredibly helpful. You can use some of the wording found in the OOH for descriptions of jobs you have held in the past, as well as for the job you are now seeking. Another good exercise is to go to potential employers' web sites and print job announcements that interest you. This is a great source for ideas and wording to include in your resume.

When you sit down to write your resume, use the job description or announcement as a guide. Focus yourself on the employer's stated requirements. First, inventory the knowledge you have that will be of greatest interest. (You will probably need to write more than one resume if you are applying for more than one job - you always want it tailored to the needs of the company you are applying with.) Second, make a list of your skills relative to the needs of the companies or industry in which you are applying. Third, make a list of your activities that relate to your career or job choice.

*Limit your resume to one page unless you are applying for an academic position.* This is easier than you might think. Use half-inch margins on the top, bottom, and sides in order to get maximum use of your page. Format your header (name, address, phone, email) horizontally and limit it to the top one-inch of the page.

*In the body of your resume put an objective.* This is a focal point and the "controller device" on your resume. Your objective must relate to the employer's needs before you will be considered for anything. (Anything that does not relate should be left off of your resume). It should be simple and concise. *For example: Objective: A position in Civil Engineering.*

*Things following your objective are put on to the resume in descending order of importance.* The next thing that goes on your resume after the objective depends on what you learn is the most important thing you have to offer the employer. This rule is followed for each and every subsequent item. Your skills are usually the most important item and are usually placed first.

*Remember that a resume is a summary of who you are.* It should tell an employer who you are and that you're "right" for the position. It must be extremely well organized and well formatted to have the greatest impact. The resume should not go on forever. The purpose of a resume is to gain the attention of the employer you hope will hire you. It is a professional statement of what you have to offer. It should be brief and concise.

*Resumes of recent college graduates should include the following master categories:*

- Objective
- Education
- Knowledge and Skills
- Project Experience (this might be merged with related experience)
- Related Experience (meaning related to your objective)
- Other Work Experience (such as food service; this section might be left out)
- Professional Activities and Accomplishments

This list of seven items works for just about every new graduate I have worked with, regardless of major.

*Resumes of experienced professionals should include the following master categories:*

- Career Objective
- Qualifications Summary
- Knowledge and Skills (this section might be left out)
- Related Work Experience
- Education, Licenses, & Certification
- Professional Activities and Accomplishments

*Rules for resume writing:*

- Limit your resume to one page.
- Include only items that support your objective.
- Use only one font for the entire resume.
- Use bold, italics, and upper case letters judiciously.
- Bold all of your master category headers in upper case letters.
- Bold all of your sub-category headers in lower case letters.
- Use action verbs to describe your experience.
- Don't use I, me or my on your resume if you can avoid it.

The above provides a complete guide for preparing your resume. But to make sense of this process, you really need to look at some samples. These samples are all templates (use in Google Docs or download to Word) that you can adapt for your uses. These are all effective resumes, resumes that actually worked in helping people land the jobs they wanted.

# 9.1 RESUME SAMPLES

SAMPLE SKILLS LIST - *Christine Green, Entrepreneur, City Girls Group & Manager, Caltrans*

SAMPLE RESUME #1 - *Project Manager*

SAMPLE RESUME #2 - *Manufacturing & Development Engineer*

SAMPLE RESUME #3 - *Electrical Power Engineer*

SAMPLE RESUME #4 - *Entry-Level Position Retail Management*

SAMPLE RESUME #5 - *Dietitian Assistant*

SAMPLE RESUME #6 - *International Business Administration*

SAMPLE RESUME #7 - *Masters Engineering-Electrical & Electronic*

SAMPLE RESUME #8 - *Legal Secretary*

SAMPLE RESUME #9 - *Sales & Marketing*

SAMPLE RESUME #10 - *Facilities Manager*

SAMPLE RESUME #11 - *Event Planning*

SAMPLE RESUME #12 - *Recreation Planning*

SAMPLE RESUME #13 - *Criminal Justice*

SAMPLE RESUME #14 - *Speech Pathology*

SAMPLE RESUME #15 - *Sales Operations Analyst*

SAMPLE RESUME #16 - *Electrical / Electronic Engineering*

SAMPLE RESUME #17 - *Computer Engineering*

SAMPLE RESUME #18 - *Computer Science*

# SAMPLE TRANSFERRABLE SKILLS LIST

## MANAGING AND LEADING

making decisions

motivating others

organizing people

coordinating a large scale project

coordinating responsibilities of others

delegating responsibilities

managing a team

## ANALYSIS AND RESEARCH

talking with experts

gathering information

interviewing experts

developing a criteria

analyzing information gathered relative to criteria

## PHYSICAL ABILITIES

athletic

enjoys the outdoors

physical stamina

manual dexterity

eye-hand coordination

## PLANNING AND ORGANIZING

developing a time line

developing a plan

organizing a schedule

attending to details

scheduling time

setting a goal

identifying tasks and activities

developing checklists

## COMMUNICATION

communicating effectively

giving clear and concise instructions

explaining information clearly

written technical communication

## ETHICS AND MORALITY

giving fair treatment to others

rational decision making

environmentally sensitive

social awareness

# MARLIN B. PROJECT MANAGER

2433 NE Sesame Street • Miami, FL 33180 • (555) 331-0756 • goldj@email.net

CAREER OBJECTIVE:   A Project Manager position in software implementation or related field.

SUMMARY OF QUALIFICATIONS:
- Managed projects ranging from $100,000 to $2,000,000
- Managed multidiscipline technical teams engaged in software development and implementation projects
- Implemented Projects for Retail, Commercial, Government, and Utility Industries, which included Nordstrom,

RELATED SKILLS:
*Computers*: Microsoft Visual Basic 6.0 • SQL 7 • Microsoft Project 98 & 2000 • ORCA & IgraphW (Delta Controls) • AutoCAD • Mechanical Desktop • TK Solver • MS DOS • Win 3.1, 95, 98, NT, & 2000 (Server and Pro) • Networking • FORTRAN • HTML & ASP • Q-basic • MS Office 97 & 2000

RELATED EXPERIENCE:

*Project Manager*              SILICON ENERGY, ALAMEDA                      12/99 – Present

Responsible for coordinating all project activities including bidding, communication with the customers and all internal communication. Plan for and support all implementation services provided to the customer, which include training, data conversion and migration, business process review and procedural modifications, technical support, and corporate interfaces. Working with the customers to identify and document their requirements in the form of action plans, work process changes and software changes. Testing and verify that the delivered products and integration software meet the customers defined requirements.

*Control Engineer (Supervisor)*       AIRCON-ENERGY, SACRAMENTO              09/98 - 12/99

Responsible for managing customer control systems, which included installed, upgraded, and troubleshooting all aspects of remote site control systems. Designed, developed, and implemented working drawings to be used by sub-contractors. Implemented and developed graphics design software program using macros and VBA. Increased graphic design productivity by more than 80%. Developed and maintained spreadsheets for the increased productivity in estimation and marketing. Design experience with Title 24, Trace 600, and energy analysis programs. Developed, designed, and implemented custom AutoCAD menus, lisps routings, and blocks, which decrease designing, time.

OTHER EXPERIENCE:

| | | |
|---|---|---|
| *CAD Designer* | IRISH COMMUNICATIONS CO., SACRAMENTO | 10/96-10/98 |
| *Pipefittter* | FILLNER CONSTRUCTION, INC, WEST SACRAMENTO | 3/94 – 12/95 |
| *Service Technician* | HUFFY SERVICE FIRST, SACRAMENTO | 7/91-3/94 |
| *Field Foreman* | TAIT ENVIRONMENTAL SERVICES, ORANGE, CA | 10/87-7/91 |

EDUCATION:
*Bachelor of Science,* Mechanical Engineering Technology
California State University, Sacramento; December 1999

*Maintained a 3.5 GPA while working 30 to 40 hours per week*

# PHILIP D. ENGINEER

9812 Blackhawk Dr. Sacramento, CA 95865 • (919) 555-1212 • engineer@yahoo.com

OBJECTIVE: A Manufacturing and Development Engineering Position with HP ProCurve

## QUALIFICATIONS SUMMARY
8 Years progressively responsible experience managing and leading new product development
• Achieved millions in cost savings through streamlined engineering processes.
• Leadership role in identifying process improvements associated with product introductions.
• Ability to prioritize and handle urgent matters effectively.
• Extensive experience working with suppliers, partners and manufacturers to ensure smooth manufacturing operations.
• Excellent communication skills. Highly organized, results oriented, and motivated by new challenges.

Software: Cadence PCB layout • Mentor Graphics • MS Office • Logic Works • P-Spice • ORCAD • Simulink • Spectra UNIX/LINUX/VI • VISIO • WINBOARD • WINDRAFT Programming: ATL • C • PROCOMM for DOS and Windows • Visual Basic • Assembly • MATLAB • PALASM

## EXPERIENCE
*Senior Product Test Engineer Qimonda*                                      3/04 - Present

Product test lead for semiconductor and PCB assembly products. Defined articulate milestones, created aggressive schedules, and planned development resources for fast moving projects. Achieved millions in cost savings through introduction of increased parallel testing, test modes, and Test Time Reduction (TTR). Prioritized new product introduction, validation, and urgent program changes, keeping production shipments on schedule. Developed power, timing and thermal characterization testing. Managed document control for multiple products. Analyzed design and test problems to solve production and customer specific issues. Improved multi-threaded programs using the CVS change control management systems, saving test time and improving code reliability. Led communications with an international design and production team to create test coverage for new products.Designed, developed, and maintained subsystems, user interface and drivers for automated testers. Mentored new and transitioning engineers.

*Manufacturing/Test Engineer Spirent Communications*                        7/02 – 9/03

Responsible for lean production test, compliance, documentation, assembly, and failure analysis for over 40 products. Transitioned all manufacturing to subcontractors. Entered schematics and PCB layouts for multiple projects. Work with test engineering and test validation groups to create test plans and procedures. Solved test and assembly problems pertaining to the transition of all service assurance products from Anritsu to Spirent, and communicated the solutions to the rest of the team. Knowledge of TCP/IP networks, streaming and control protocols

*Manufacturing/Test Engineer Anritsu Corporation*                           9/00 – 7/02

Designed test fixture, program, and procedure for power supplies, controllers, and telecommunications access products. UsingTL1 commands, developed test platforms for DS1 test and access equipment. Trained technicians to use test equipment; including logic analyzers and oscilloscopes. Conducted monthly failed parts meeting. In charge of compliance testing including EMC, environmental and vibration testing. Part of new product development team for 5 separate projects, including TCP/IP controller. Lead component engineer in charge of solutions for alternate sources, replacement circuits, and lifecycle requirements. Liaison to contract manufacturers, troubleshooting problems and resolving issues.

*Senior Design Project*                                                      10/99 – 5/00

Leader of a team of 3 engineers in the design, fabrication, and evaluation of a wireless motorized cart. The cart uses phase and signal strength to follow a transmitter placed on the user. Personally responsible for project coordination and integration throughout the one-year project.

## EDUCATION:
*Bachelor of Science, Electronic & Electrical Engineering* • CSU, Sacramento May 2000
*Professional Training:* Wireless Communications including Klystron Theory, Fiber Optics, Financial Management

# TIKAN SINGH

1234 Electric Avenue, #100, Sacramento, CA 95815 (916) 555-1234 tikans@email.com

OBJECTIVE: A position in Electrical Power Engineering.

## EDUCATION

*Bachelor of Science*, Electrical Power Engineering, California State University, Sacramento GPA -3.43 May 2010
*Power Certificate*, California State University, Sacramento May 2010
*Accepted for Fall 2010: Master of Science*, Electrical Power Engineering, California State University, Sacramento
*Engineer-In-Training Certified*, National Council of Examiners for Engineering and Surveying
Dean's Honor List

## RELATED COURSEWORK

| | | |
|---|---|---|
| Power System Relay Protection | Analysis of Faulted Power Systems | Transmission Lines |
| Power System Analysis | Advanced Topics in Power Systems | Network Analysis |
| Electric Power Distribution | Energy System Control and Optimization | Circuit Analysis |
| Electromechanical Conversion | Control Systems and Feedback | Electronics I |

## PROJECTS

Sr. Projects-6 month projects involving project proposal, design specs, weekly status updates, comprehensive report and presentation.

*Sr. Project 1: Fault Analysis* –Lead a team of four to analyze shunt faults in a six-bus system. Sequence and Phase Fault currents, voltages were calculated and compared to ASPEN simulations at all the bus sites.

*Sr. Project 2*: Relay Protection –Leading a four-member team that is designing relay protection for a power system. Calculation of relay settings and their coordination with other relays are being designed and then will be verified with ASPEN simulation.*

*Circuit Designing:* Built circuits using resistors, diodes, operational amplifiers, digital multimeter, function generator, oscilloscope, and tested them on MultiSim, PSpice. Wrote reports in compliance with IEEE standards.

## SOFTWARE SKILLS

ASPEN • Matlab • Orcad PSpice •ADS • MultiSim • JMP • MS Visio • MS Office Suite ASP.Net • PLSQL • SQL Server 2008 • C# • C • HTML

## EXPERIENCE

*Student Assistant Employment Development Department*, Sacramento, CA                06/2009- Present

Created a website using the service-oriented architecture to automate tax seminar customer registration on the Employment Development Department website. Visual Studio 2008, SQL Server 2008, and Team Foundation Server were employed for the application.

*Design Validation Intern Intel Corporation,* Folsom, CA                06/2008 – 05/2009

• Created a tool that notifies engineers of out of spec thermal data saving hundreds of annual hours of labor. This tool uses the SQL to link to the Oracle database from a Matlab platform to generate reports.
• Designed a tool that reports the frequency response of different power states of the processors to Intel customers. Matlab and Steffensens-theorem were used to generate the charts and generate reports over a period of three months.
• Planned and developed a tool to generate reports on efficiency of testers and head-count usage. Upper management uses this tool to allocate resources in a more efficient way.
• Created an automated tool for four separate teams of Engineering Operations to reduce redundancy in standard work ordering.

# CATHY FLYNN

555 25th Avenue, #1, San Francisco 94121 • 916.555.1212 • catherine.flynn@email.com

OBJECTIVE: An entry-level position in retail management.

## STRENGTHS
- Exceptional team and leadership skills
- Well refined communication skills
- Excellent customer service skills
- Able to adapt rapidly to new situations and new cultures

## EDUCATION
*Bachelor of Science in Commerce*, Business Management • Santa Clara University • May 2005 • GPA 3.3

## RELATED COURSES
Foundations of Business Leadership Management Information Systems
Business Leadership Skills Financial Management Skills
Business Ethics Industrial Relations
Organization and Management Information for Business Decisions I & II
Organizational Structure Design Statistics and Data Analysis I & II

## KNOWLEDGE & SKILLS
*Leadership/ Team:* Skilled at motivating team members by identifying individual strengths and delegating responsibilities. Able to effectively coach individuals and groups to improve performance and skills. Experience explaining complex ideas and concepts in easily understandable language.
*Communication/ Customer Service:* Effective in social situations, interacting easily with new people and establishing rapport. Experience working with customers to identify needs and make appropriate product and service recommendations. Skilled at defusing problems and resolving complaints to reach desired customer satisfaction.
*Organization:* Knowledge of organizational management developed through business management coursework. Experience coordinating people and resources in order to put a plan into effect and meet specific deadlines. Able to work under pressure in a high stress, fast paced environment where accuracy is essential.

## EXPERIENCE
*Assistant Account Coordinator Tutti Fruitti Promotions*, Sydney, Australia
12/06 to 5/07
Reported directly to the president and management team to plan and oversee promotions for shopping centers. Organized events, redesigned shopping center logos, and provided excellent customer service.

*Captain/ Team Player New South Wales Water Polo Club*, Sydney, Australia
12/05 to 5/07
Team captain and competitor for a water polo club at the highest level of competition in Australia. Led the team to its highest ranking in the club's history. Also responsible for running water polo camps, school leagues, and community activities.

*Assistant Manager Arbors Apartment Complex*, Davis, CA                6/06 to 10/06
Negotiated contracts and handled lease agreements. Showcased model apartments and responded to inquiries. Resolved resident complaints and maintenance issues efficiently and effectively.

## ACTIVITIES & ACCOMPLISHMENTS
- Senior Leadership Academy, Santa Clara University
- Member, Student Athletic Advisory Committee
- Captain, Water Polo Team, Santa Clara University
- Experience traveling and living internationally and adapting to other cultures

# BEV QUINTO

1931 Sesame St. Apt. 90, Sacramento, CA 95825 • (555) 555-0341 • bev@email.net

**OBJECTIVE:**   A position as a Dietetic Assistant.

**EDUCATION:**
*In progress: Bachelor of Science,* Dietetics • CSU Sacramento • To Be Completed: May 2010.

**RELATED COURSES:**
Medical Nutrition Therapy I Community Nutrition* Food Management
Medical Nutrition Therapy II Nutrition and Metabolism Food Service Management
Nutrition in the Lifespan Advanced Nutrition and Metabolism Cultural and Social Aspects of Food
Nutrition and Wellness Food Safety and Sanitation Principle of Food Preparation

**CERTIFICATES:**
*ServSafe Certification:* April 2007

**SKILLS:**
*Communication:*
• Comfortable speaking to groups and explaining complex information in an easy understandable language
• Exceptional writing skills; experience writing reports and creating PowerPoint presentations
• Interact with the public to provide information about food health issues
• Skilled at giving presentations using visual aids
*Research and Analysis:*
• Skilled at using nutritional formulas to calculate clients' needs
• Experienced researching for information through library data bases such as PubMed and EBSCOhost
*Computer Skills:*
Operating Systems: Windows XP/2000/98/95 • Macintosh OSX
Software: Diet Analysis plus 8.0, MS Word, Excel, PowerPoint, Filemaker Pro,

**WORK EXPERIENCE:**
*Student Assistant ECS Career Services*, CSU Sacramento                              11/04 - present
Train and manage student assistant team. Maintain and update computer database systems such as Filemaker Pro
and Excel files. Help edit weekly newsletters written by the Director of Career Services. Responsible for maintaining office operations when the Director of Career Services is absent throughout summer.

*Nutrition Aide Meals For Life Coach* – Sacramento                              1/08 - present
Working in a team environment to help prepare a week's worth of meals and snacks given to at least 7 clients.
Adhere to food safety and sanitation while preparing and packaging meals and snacks. Responsible for delivering
items to clients when supervisor is absent.

*Intern University Of California Cooperative Extension,* San Joaquin County          2/08 – present
Provide nutritional information to low-income families. Projects include: creation of PowerPoint presentation for
nutrition classes and organizing nutrition packets.

*Student Assistant California Department of Public Health-* WIC Branch              6/07 – 8/07
Helped develop survey questions for food buying practices, food consumption, and preferences of WIC participants. Traveled statewide to WIC clinics to administer survey to WIC participants.

# JACK GOLDSON

2433 NE Sesame Street Miami, FL 33180 • (555) 331-0756 • goldj@email.net

## QUALIFICATIONS SUMMARY:

- Managed organizations with staffs of 45 to 350, and budgets ranging from $1m to $5m, involving all areas of business: production, administration, personnel, accounting, finance, sales & marketing.
- Skilled at motivating and training personnel and developing human resources.
- 15 years experience in turning around operations from deficit to profitability and growth.
- Significant experience in international environment operating businesses profitability under different cultures and legal systems: Colombia, Hungary, USA.
- Developed and implemented operational procedures and quality standards in order to obtain first SGS certifications in Colombia for companies in Floriculture and Hotel Industries.

## PROFESSIONAL EXPERIENCE

*General Director (President)  Lancaster House* Bogota, Colombia, 2001-present
Direct all areas of operation for an upscale apart-hotel complex offering conference rooms, restaurants, bar, gym/sauna, and business center. Catering primarily to both foreign and domestic corporate accounts. Implemented software package increasing efficiency, profits, and image. Turned around operation from delegated/franchise management to self-managed. Improved occupancy from 45% to 75%, increased average daily rate by close to 100%, and raised net return by over 100%.

*Chief Executuive Officer Flora Intercontinental* Bogota, Colombia 1991-2006
Served as CEO of flower growing and exporting farms, selling close to 25 million roses a year or about 2% of total US rose market. Took operation from 25 acres and near bankruptcy in 1991 to profitability, with 78 acres under greenhouse, and final sale of company in 2006. Developed exporting markets in USA, Canada, Europe, and South America via traditional wholesalers and supermarkets channels. As member of various boards and committees in the industry, organized social and environmental programs for people in floriculture, designed marketing campaigns abroad, lobbied before various US Government offices in Washington. Instrumental in defeating anti-dumping class action suit against Colombian rose growers before the US Department of Commerce in 1994.

## ELECTED POSITIONS AND ACCOMPLISHMENTS

- *Board of Directors, Asocolflores*: 1997-2004. Served two years as Vice President of the Association of Colombian Flower growers and exporters, with over 220 members representing interests in Colombia and abroad for the country's second largest agricultural export product after coffee, with sales of close to USD 1B and over 80,000 direct employees.
- *Board of Directors, Colombia Flower Council (CFC)*: 2000-2006. Association based in Miami, representing the interest of the Colombian Flower Industry at a City, State and National Level.
- *Board of Directors, Flower Promotion Organization (FPO)*: 2000-2004. Program sponsored by US and Colombian flower growers destined to develop the general consumption of flowers in the US market.
- *Marketing Committee, Society of American Florists (SAF)*: 2003-2005 Various Marketing campaigns for largest umbrella organization for the Flower Industry in the US
- Ranked 2nd/ 60,000 students nationwide in ICFES college entrance examinations, Colombia 1986

## EDUCATION

*Bachelor of Science in Economics*, Cum Laude
The Wharton School of Business, University of Pennsylvania, Philadelphia, 1991
    Majored in Entrepreneurial Management and International Finance

## RELATED SKILLS:

Computers: Word, Excel, Internet applications
Multilingual: Spanish/English/Hebrew/Hungarian

# SCOTT SONG

2357 Sesame Street, Apt. G105, Sacramento, CA 95825 • (555) 555-4797 • songs@email.com

OBJECTIVE:   A position in Electrical/Computer Engineering

## EDUCATION

*In progress: Master of Science, Electrical and Electronic Engineering*, CSU-Sacramento Expected May 2008
*Master of Science, Mechanical Engineering*, CSU-Sacramento, GPA 3.84/4.00 May 2004
*Bachelor of Science, Mechanical Engineering*, Chung Yuan Christian University, Taiwan June 1997

## RELATED COURSES

Analog and Mixed Signal IC Design Electronics I & II Physical Electronics
Advanced Semiconductor Devices CMOS and VLSI Design Modern Communication Systems
Numerical Methods Digital Control Systems Intro to Feedback Systems
Digital Control of Manufacturing Processes Transmission Line and Fields Robotics

## SKILLS

*Computer Software & Hardware Applications*
PSPICE • L-Edit • Matlab • Labview – Virtual Instrumentation • SX-Key • Intel vPro Technology • Needham SPI Programmer • Altiris • LANDesk • Microsoft SMS • Micorsoft Virtual Server • VMware Workstation WS-FTP • PLC • AutoCAD • Neuro-Fuzzy Systems • Microsoft Office • Windows OS • MS-DOS • Macintosh
*Communication/Organization*
• Bilingual: English/Chinese(Mandarin)
• Excellent technical writing and presentation skills
• Excellent problem solving and analytical skills

## PROJECTS

*Transfer Thin-Film Silicon to Flexible Substrate Using Adhesive Bonding and Wet Etching (EE Master Thesis)*: Developed a method to bond SOI wafer to a plastic material using BCB polymer as the adhesion. Conventional wet etching was then carried out to thin silicon substrate using an etchant with higher etch rate in order to get thin-film silicon on the flexible substrate.

*CMOS and VLSI Design:* Design and layout of the error-correction and decode logic circuit for a 3-stage 1.5bit/stage pipelined ADC. The aspect ratio was adjusted by equalizing fall time and rise time of each gate, and the mask layout was finished according to the calculated ratio. The size of the circuit was optimized by minimizing the area in the layout.

*Audio Amplifier for Headsets:* Member of a four-person team that designed a circuit to amplify audio signal through a headphone. Simulation was made using PSPICE. Actual circuit was built and stress and sensitivity analysis were performed.

*Intelligent Monitoring of Turning Tools (ME Master's Thesis):* Developed a technique for monitoring tool wear and tool conditions during turning operations. Data was collected using a PC with data acquisition board and Labview virtual instruments. BPN of Explore Net and ANFIS of Matlab were used for analysis. A successful prediction of tool wear was achieved.

## WORK EXPERIENCE

*Graduate Intern Technical Platform Application Engineering*, Intel Corporation 8/06 – 8/07
Worked on PAE AMT debug team supporting OEM/ODM sightings investigation of manageability engine and Intel Active Management Technology components. Responsibilities include debugging customer issues, conducting platform basic acceptance testing, developing documents of tools user guide and lab network topology, setting up ISV servers in enterprise network, and running ISV use case testing.

## ACCOMPLISHMENT AND ACTIVITIES

President, Taiwan Student Association, CSU-Sacramento (2001 ~ 2002)

# CHRISTINE WROBLE

6100 Sesame Park Dr., College Park, MD 20740 • 301-555-5555 • cwrobl@email.com

OBJECTIVE: A legal secretary position.

## QUALIFICATIONS SUMMARY
- 20+ years experience as a legal secretary.
- Highly skilled at quality document production including formatting, editing, revising, document comparison and final
  document production.
- 10 years experience in corporate merger.
- 6 years experience in government affairs.
- Able to work effectively with multiple legal professionals simultaneously, coordinating schedules, conference calls, managing calendars, and maintaining complex filing systems.
- Extensive experience with complex legal billing.
- Detail-oriented, very well organized and able to work independently.

## COMPUTER/TECHNICAL SKILLS:
*Document Creation Software:* MS Word, Excel, and PowerPoint • Windows XP, MacPac  Schedule Management: MS Outlook • WebElite • *Time EntryMarketing Software: InterAction Web Client
*Record Management Software*: FileSurf

## PROFESSIONAL EXPERIENCE
*Legal Secretary Time Warner,* Washington, DC                                    1/09 – present
Temporary employee responsible for providing clerical services to four attorneys.

*Legal Secretary DLA Piper LLP* (US), Washington, DC
1/00 – 10/08
Worked for Of Counsel and two Associates in Government Affairs Group with responsibilities for timely entry of attorney time; type correspondence and memoranda; handle client phone calls; manage filing of all correspondence on a daily basis; arrange conference calls and meetings. Previously worked for 2 Associates in Corporate Group. Coordinated assembly of closing documents for clients; worked with client in keeping records of client's employees for stock reasons and issued stock certificates to retired/terminated employees.

*Legal Secretary Akin, Gump, Strauss, Hauer & Feld, L.L.P.*, Washington, DC
1/90 –12/99
Responsible for timely entry of attorney time; managed client billings; typed correspondence and memoranda; effectively handled large volume of client phone calls; managed filing of all correspondence and documents on a daily basis; arranged conference calls and meetings; distributed work when partner was away.

*Legal Secretary Sidley & Austin*, Washington, DC                                2/89 – 12/89
Started as a temporary in February 1989. Offered permanent position in March 1989 in Antitrust and Litigation Sections. Prepared motions, correspondence and memoranda; responsible for timely entry of attorney time; handled large volumes of client phone calls; responsible for filing on a daily basis.

## EDUCATION
*Strayer University* – Washington, DC 1996 – 1998 • Courses in Computer Information Systems
*St Helena Business High School*, Bronx, New York • Secretarial/ Business Courses

# LESLIE SCHNEIDER

820 Sesame Street, Burlingame, CA 94101 • (650) 555.157 • LeslieS@email.com

OBJECTIVE: A Sales Development Representative position with Marketo

STRENGTHS:
- Exceptional sales development skills
- Skilled at prospecting, lead development, customer cultivation and follow-up
- Experienced in account/sales management
- Highly motivated and charismatic
- Adept at business prospect research and analysis

*RELATED KNOWLEDGE & SKILLS:*
*Communication/Customer Service:* Connect easily and effectively with new people and quickly establish rapport. Experience interacting with customers requiring information, service or help on a continual basis. Possess excellent writing skills. Able to accurately document sales activities, and create effective business documents, correspondence and written communications.

*Marketing/Sales:* Skilled at quickly identifying customer needs and preferences and making appropriate product and service recommendations. Excellent team player with the ability to negotiate effectively to reach desired results and corporate goals. Enjoy the process of prospecting, educating and qualifying customers. Able to maintain incredibly positive attitude and create new business opportunities.

*Organization:* Experienced in researching accounts, identifying key players, and creating demand. Works well with other team members.

RELATED EXPERIENCE:
*Part-time Manager,* ALD Investments, San Mateo, CA                    1999-current
Manage property, construction projects and large scale remodels for small development company. Interact with leasing brokers, potential tenants and vendors. Coordinate repairs. Market properties to potential buyers.

*Account Executive, MSA Industries, So San Francisco, CA,*              1988-1999
Managed outside sales territory and coordinated sales team; researched, identified new business and developed cold leads into multi-million dollar contracts; and created a new vertical market in Silicon Valley selling directly to end-users for MSA Industries the nation's largest supplier and installer of floor coverings. In 1997 DuPont Corporation acquired MSA.

*Inside Sales Representative, Virtual Microsystems, Berkeley, CA*        1986-1988
Managed Mid-West territory; canvassed DEC sales people to co-develop territory for Virtual Microsystems a company that manufactured and sold CD ROM Multi-processors that allowed simultaneous access of PC programs from VAX terminals.

*Marketing Representative,* Wang Laboratories, San Francisco, CA         1984-1986
Managed sales and installation (with Senior Sales Representative and partner), handling key accounts including Bank of California, Wells Fargo Bank and Crocker Bank for Wang Laboratories, a leader in word processing and IT systems. Achieved sales quota first year. Developed into a trusted account manager for multiple banks. Cold called non-Wang accounts.

EDUCATION:
*BA, Political Science, Minor: Business; UCLA, 1984*

# DAVID MITTO

2830 Ash Avenue, Sacramento, CA 95821 • (916) 555-5555 • mitto@email.com

OBJECTIVE: A position in operations, facilities and project management.

## SUMMARY OF QUALIFICATIONS
- 15 years experience in the direct management of all phases of industrial operations, safety, and security and project management.
- Skilled at providing effective leadership for a large-scale operations, department and organization, working cooperatively with all departments.
- Extensive experience managing internal police/security, operations superintendents, and operations personnel.
- Developed emergency, security and threat assessment plan for complex facility.
- Developed and refined comprehensive safety training, accident, illness and prevention program for multi-department facility.
- Directed grant writing resulting in federal funding bringing large-scale facility into compliance with Homeland Security regulations.

## RELATED EXPERIENCE
*Asst. Manager Northern California Operations: Metropolitan Corporation*     03/05 – present
*Director of Operations: Port of Sacramento*, Sacramento     12/91 – 03/05

Plan, direct, supervise and coordinate all phases of operational activities and security for large-scale multi-faceted facility. Responsible for terminal operations, overseeing provisional services to customers, including tenants, stevedores, steamship companies, trucking, and railroad entities. Represent the organization with various federal and state safety, labor, and security entities in matters pertaining to operations. Manage and develop safety programs designed to provide a safe work environment for all personnel and customers. Facilitate inspections and coordinate a response to the U. S. Coast Guard, Office of Safety and Health Administration and other federal, state and local agencies. Implement law and regulation changes. Coordinate with the facility engineer on capital improvements and major maintenance work to maximize customer service and safety. Serve as the chief negotiator for the development of labor agreements, working with legal counsel and other affected department directors. Collaborate with the marketing department to advance business development. Maintain weekly schedules.

## EMPLOYMENT HISTORY
*Asst. Manager Northern California Operations Metropolitan Corporation*     03/05 – present
*Director of Operations Port of Sacramento*     12/91 – 03/05
*West Coast Asst. Operations Manager Star Shipping (U.S.W.C.), Inc.*     02/85 – 12/91
*Marine Superintendent Marine Terminals Corporation*     09/84 – 02/85
*Licensed Third Mate Global Marine Co., Inc.*     03/83 – 05/83
*Licensed Third Mate Masters, Mates, and Pilots Union*     08/80 – 03/83

## EDUCATION
Bachelor of Science Industrial Technology • CalPoly • San Luis Obispo • June 1980
*Professional and Continuing Education*
Hazardous Wastes Manifest Training • Metropolitan Corporation • Wilmington, California • September 2006
Home Land Security Facility Training • California Maritime Academy • Vallejo, California • November 2005
Effective Negotiating Techniques • Scott Works • San Francisco, California • Spring 1989
International Transportation • Golden Gate University • San Francisco, CA • Fall 1985
Second Mates License – Unlimited, any Tonnage • United State Coast Guard • 1983
Labor Relations Training, International Law • United States Naval Reserve • 1982 and 1983

# STEPHANIE ZIM

PO Box 55512, Sacramento, CA • 916-555-5555 • szim@email.com

OBJECTIVE: A position in conference planning.

## QUALIFICATION SUMMARY
- 3.5 years progressively responsible experience in customer service
- Highly effective in maintaining positive customer relations
- Skilled at helping customers identify and meet goals
- Able to anticipate, manage, and troubleshoot problems effectively and efficiently
- Excellent communication skills; create deliver effective written communications and PowerPoint presentations

## EDUCATION

*Bachelor of Science, Business Administration*; Concentration: Finance • CSU, Sacramento • GPA 3.4 • May 2006

## RELATED COURSES:
Principles of Marketing Strategic Management Legal Environment of Business
Salesmanship Management of Contemporary Financial Accounting
Market Analysis & Feasibility Studies Organizations Managerial Accounting
Operations Management Computer Information Systems for Business Finance

## KNOWLEDGE & SKILLS
*Organization and Time Management*
- Experience assisting with all aspects of conference planning, coordination, and delivery
- Excellent planning and time management skills; able to break large projects into manageable components
- Able to work independently taking initiative to meet goals and expectations
- Able to work effectively in a team environment both as a leader and as a productive team member

*Communication*
- Well-refined written, verbal and presentation skills
- Exceptional customer service skills; able to make appropriate recommendations to help customers meet goals

*Computer*
- Macintosh and PC Systems * PowerPoint, Excel, Word * Filemaker Pro * Outlook
- Adapt quickly to new environments and technologies

## EMPLOYMENT
*Office Assistant*                                               1/2005 to 6/2006
Career Services Office, College of Engineering and Computer Science, CSUS
Helped coordinate and deliver multiple large-scale career events with up 350 corporate and government representatives and 1500 students and alumni. Developed excellent communication, organization, and time management skills working independently with minimal supervision on a wide variety of tasks in a fast paced environment. Developed customer service skills working with students and employers by identifying needs and providing accurate information.

*Financial/ Investment Advisor*                                 7/2006 to Present
Wells Fargo Financial Services
Provide financial advice to customers by identifying individual needs and goals necessary to achieve objectives. Interacting effectively with customers to develop financial plans, and make investment, life insurance, and long term care product service recommendations. Research investment options and make suitable recommendations to customers. Maintain risk awareness and regulatory knowledge.

# JULIE J. MCHALE

9999 Morning Mews.Columbia, MD • 12345 • 555-555-5555 • jmchale@greenbelt.gov

OBJECTIVE: A position as director of recreation for the city of Greenbelt that allows me make a positive difference in the community.

## PROFESSIONAL QUALIFICATIONS
- 25+ years of experience in managing city-wide recreation programs
- Extensive experience managing budgets, resources, and staff
- Highly skilled in finding and applying for appropriate grant money to enhance existing programs
- Extensive experience in developing innovative programs to meet the needs of a diverse multigenerational population
- Excellent communication and presentation skills

## EXPERIENCE
*Assistant Director of Recreation Greenbelt Recreation Department*                                    2001-present
Responsible for execution and overall fiscal management of the Recreation budget and presenting findings to City Council. Serve as liaison on various committees and boards. Increased revenues in program budgets by over 20% in last three years. Continuously build and nurture valuable partnerships throughout Greenbelt. Support 'going green', twenty-first century marketing. Increased attendance in recreation programs by 10% in each of the last three years. Created the "Get Active Greenbelt" a leading program in the area of community health and wellness. Developed and administer "Be Happy, Be Healthy Employee Health and Wellness Program" which serves as a model throughout the country.

*Recreation Supervisor Greenbelt Recreation Department*                                    1997-2001
Supervised, provided leadership and encouraged a 'team management style' approach to 5 full-time and over 80 part time employees. Responsible for the design, coordination and distribution of the quarterly brochure for all department wide events the major recreation advertisement. Developed and implemented training courses for program staff. Assisted with the promotion of citywide events through the budgeting, planning, development and implementation of the department's self-supporting annual events.

*Recreation Coordinator Greenbelt Recreation Department*                                    1985-1997
Assisted with recruitment of staff, development and implementation of all self supporting programs to including special events, camps and classes. Assisted in the purchasing and proper care, use and maintenance of equipment and facilities.

## EDUCATION AND CERTIFICATION
BS Health, Physical Education and Recreation • Slippery Rock University, Slippery Rock PACertified Parks and Recreation Professional •1989 • National Recreation and Parks Association

## PROFESSIONAL ACTIVITIES & ACCOMPLISHMENTS
- Awarded Government Citation for the Get Active Greenbelt program, March 2009
- Special Recognition, Maryland Recreation and Parks Association for "Be Happy, Be Healthy Program," April 2009
- State and National Presenter and Resource, community and employee health and wellness/recreation programming, 2007
- Vice President, Maryland Recreation and Parks Association, 2004
- Vice President, Maryland Municipal League Recreation Branch, 1999-present

# NICO GILBERT-IGELSRUD

9257 Elm Street, Sacramento, CA, 95826 • nicogilbertigelsrud@email.com • (123) 574-3800

**OBJECTIVE**: An internship in Criminal Justice.

## STRENGTHS
- Effective leadership skills developed through lead student assistant and poll inspector positions
- Exceptional interpersonal skills; able to work as an effective team member and team lead
- Well-refined research and compilation skills; able to identify and organize critical information
- Able to create and deliver effective presentations

## EDUCATION
In progress: BS, Criminal Justice; Minor: Middle East & Islamic Studies
CSU Sacramento • December 2013

## COURSE WORK
General Investigative Techniques • Law of Arrest, Search, and Seizure • Law of Crimes
Structure and Function of American Courts • Police and Society • Justice and Public Safety
Administration • Middle East Societies and Culture • Intro to Physical Evidence • Elementary Arabic
Drug Abuse and Criminal Behavior • Gangs & Threat Groups In America • Introduction to Islam
In Progress: Sex Offenses & Offenders • Government and Politics in the Middle East

## WORK EXPERIENCE
*Lead Student Assistant ECS Career Center*                                       09/08 - present
Train, schedule, and supervise new student assistants. Work closely with ECS Career staff and employers while assisting with various office duties. Maintain job listings; edit reports and articles in the Career Services newsletter. Maintain databases pertaining to student/career information. Assist in researching and compiling workforce and salary data. Assist in analyzing and preparing data for presentation. Contact companies to collect and submit payments valued at an average of $1,000 per transaction.

*Event/Equipment Attendant The WELL*                                            06/11 – present
Work as a member of a team and individually to set up events including the World Master's Track Meet and Special Olympics basketball. Ensure that equipment and furnishings are delivered, set up, maintained and accounted for. Respond to customer questions and concerns, including VIP events and ensure positive experience for all visitors. Interview potential employees for event services. Check out equipment to students and staff. Handle product sales including cash and credit transactions.

*Poll Inspector Yolo County Elections Office*                                   10/08 – 11/10
Manage the set up and operation of a Yolo County polling place for multiple elections. Organize polling precinct for efficiency. Manage team of poll workers throughout Election Day. Assist voters with questions and concerns, troubleshooting problems throughout Election Day. Responsible for maintaining ballot integrity over course of each election, including delivering ballots from voting site to election headquarters.

*Cashier Impossible Acres Pumpkin Patch*                                        06/08 - 10/10
Opened the store in the morning and set up produce displays. Answered questions and pointing out various points of interest. Handled transactions efficiently and effectively. Closed store operations at the end of each day and secured money and equipment. Maintained a proper change count throughout the day.

## ACCOMPLISHMENTS & ACTIVITIES
Membership Coordinator • American Criminal Justice Association • Spring 2012
Chair, Social Committee • American Criminal Justice Association • Fall 2011, Spring 2013

# SARAH SPEECHPATH

1306 Sesame Street, #2, Sacramento, CA 95816 • 916-123-8803 • sarahspeechpath@email.com

OBJECTIVE: A position in speech pathology at UC Davis Medical Center.

## STRENGTHS
• Thorough knowledge of communication disorders
• Knowledge of anatomy associated with communication disorders
• Experience communicating with medical professionals at all levels regarding speech, language, and cognitive problems associated with neurogenic disorders
• Excellent verbal and written communication skills; able to communicate effectively with diverse client base
• Able to analyze phases of swallowing to identify dysphagia and identify treatment and diet modifications
• Bilingual: English/Spanish

## EDUCATION
MS Speech Pathology • CSU, Sacramento • GPA 3.9 • December 2013
BS Speech Pathology and Audiology • CSU, Sacramento • May 2013
Dean's Honor Roll

## RELATED COURSES
Dysphagia and the Medical Setting
Neurogenic Language Disorders
Motor Speech Disorders
Counseling Techniques for Speech Pathologists and Audiologists
Intro to Medical Speech Pathology
Anatomy and Physiology of the Speech Mechanism
Voice and Fluency

## LICENSURE & CERTIFICATION
Certificate of Clinical Competence Speech Language Pathology (CCC-SLP)
Speech Language Pathologist Assistant License, State of California

## RELATED EXPERIENCE
*Speech Pathology Intern UC Davis Med Center*                          5/2012 to present
Worked with inpatient acute care and out patient dysphagia clients to assess swallowing impairment, and develop strategies and/or diet modifications for safe swallow rehabilitation. Under supervision of Speech Pathologist, responsible for evaluation and treatment of motor speech disorders related to stroke, traumatic brain injury, and cancer.

*Speech Pathology Intern Jabber Gym*                          8/2011 to 10/2012
Provided early intervention for children, ages one month to eight years, with speech, language, motor and cognitive difficulties. Worked with team to evaluate, plan and provide treatment and instruction. Participated in consultations with parents to facilitate development and treatment of skills.

*Unit Assistant Mercy San Juan Med Center*                          7/2009 to 8/2011
Assist staff in contacting other medical facilities to obtain records, arrange for patient transport, and to obtain equipment and supplies. Collaborate with speech language pathologists, nurses, dietitians, and physicians for patient care. Gained exposure to trauma, neuroscience and intensive care unit patients. Developed and refined communications, team, and time management skills.

# KEVIN COWAN

2618 Sesame Street Apt. 8, Sacramento,CA 95800

OBJECTIVE: A sales operations analyst position.

## QUALIFICATION SUMMARY
• 6.5 years sales and marketing experience
• Proficient with Salesforce CRM
• Skilled at performing market research, forecasting, and trend analysis
• Able to anticipate, manage, and troubleshoot problems effectively and efficiently
• Excellent B2B representative; experienced working with wholesalers
• Excellent communication skills; create and deliver effective written communications as well as PowerPoint presentations

## EDUCATION
*Master of Business Administration, Executive Management;* • CSU, Sacramento • GPA 3.9 • Feb 2013
*Bachelor of Arts, Broadcast & Electronic Communications*; • San Francisco State University • GPA 3.5 • May 2004

## RELATED COURSES:
Strategic Analysis Global Marketing Organizational Design & Management
Quantitative Decision Making Strategic Marketing Business Finance
Project Management Leadership & Change Management Financial Accounting
Technology Management Managing Innovation & Creativity Managerial Accounting

## KNOWLEDGE & SKILLS
• Well-refined written, verbal and presentation skills
• Exceptional customer service skills; able to make appropriate recommendations to help customers meet goals
• Macintosh and PC Systems * PowerPoint, Excel, Word, OneNote * Microsoft Project * ProTools * Outlook
• Languages including Java * C * HTML * XHTML

## EMPLOYMENT

*Business Strategy Analyst*          Cowan Team (Keller Williams Realty)          8/2008 to Present
Researched and implemented cloud based CRM software (Short Sale Commander) to manage the increase in clients and lenders. Applied inventory management theories to improve the turnover rate of listings in the system by 20%, reducing the time an average listing was in the system from 71 days to 59 days. Implemented Dropbox to reduce administrative costs, improve file organization for the team, and reduce file transfer mistakes. Implemented eFaxing to expedite the short sale process, reducing response time with lenders and improving listing turnover rate. These changes were key drivers for increasing net profit by 46%, from $345,000 in 2011 to $503,000 in 2012.

*Key Account Manager*          Pyramid Breweries          2/2006 to 8/2008
Negotiated the deal between Pyramid and Plutos Restaurants to sell Pyramid beers in each Plutos location. Designed the branding for the Plutos "Atomic Ale." Brainstormed ideas with the Pluto's ownership group, and then found local vendors to turn the idea into reality. Was the B2B representative for Pyramid Breweries, working with wholesalers in Northern California. Part of a team that designed and successfully implemented a strategic sales plan to increase premiere accounts in the Bay Area by 15% in 2007. Increased brand visibility by submitting Pyramid beers to local beer competitions and tradeshows, and then championing the product by attending each event, in addition to promoting Pyramid Breweries at beer festivals in Nevada and California.

## ACTIVITIES & ACCOMPLISHMENTS
• Member of Sacramento Area Regional Technology Alliance (SARTA)
• Member of Beta Gamma Sigma Honor Society

# ERIC SPRUNG

5271 Sesame Street, Sacramento, CA 95819

OBJECTIVE: A position in Electrical / Electronic Engineering.

## EDUCATION
*B.S. Electrical and Electronic Engineering, CSU, Sacramento* - Major GPA 4.00 - December 2012
*A.S. Mathematics and Physical Science*, American River College, Sacramento - December 2005
*EIT Certified* - December 2012

## RELATED COURSES

Electronics I & Electronics II
Advanced Analog   Integrated Circuits
Physical Electronics
Product Design Project I & II

Robotics
Feedback Systems
Digital Control Systems
Network Analysis

Applied Electromagnetics
Modern Communications Systems
S ignals & Systems

## KNOWLEDGE & SKILLS
*Programming, Circuit Design, and Simulation*
• Strong programming and embedded experience - C/C++ - LabVIEW - Verilog- - Visual Basic - dsPIC - PIC18 - FPGA
• Analog / digital circuit design, simulation, and hardware experience - PSPICE - Multisim - Matlab - ADS - Ultiboard
• Graphics and documentation - MS Project - MS Visio - MS Office - Latex - Photoshop - Illustrator
*Communication, Project Management, and Organization*
• Excellent verbal and written communication skills, extensive project management and team leadership experience.
• Proven ability to learn and adapt to new technologies and situations quickly; able to work independently, coordinate multiple tasks, and resolve complex problems.

## PROJECT EXPERIENCE
*Senior Design*: Low Power Energy Harvesting Wireless Sensor System
Co-developed a wireless sensor suite powered by ambient indoor light using advanced energy harvesting circuitry and extremely low power sensors. Gained solid experience in dsPIC programming, MiWi, SPI, USB and UART communication, project management, and team leadership. Co-authored paper "Low Power-Energy Storage System for Energy Harvesting Applications" currently under review for publication in IEEE Transactions on Power Electronics. Simulation for "Optimal Autonomous UAV Motion Planning in a Dynamic World" Created a 3D vehicle simulation system in Matlab for a paper entitled "Optimal Autonomous UAV Motion Planning in a Dynamic World" in preparation for submission to IEEE Transactions on Robotics. The system uses modular, object-oriented design to track trajectories, collision detection, and optimization decisions for one UAV and four moving obstacles.

*Energy Management Demonstration Projects*
Led the development of two advanced energy management demonstration systems for the California Smart Grid Center including a Lithium-ion monitoring and control system and a digitally controlled variable load for photovoltaic maximum power point characterization. Designed supporting analog current measurement, signal conditioning, and relay circuitry.

## PROFESSIONAL EXPERIENCE
Research Engineer California Smart Grid Center 10/2010 – Present
• Led a team of three in the development of an advanced Lithium-ion battery management system using LabVIEW.

123 Sesame Street Antelope, CA 95824 • (916) 7654-321 • aml263@email.com

**OBJECTIVE:** An internship position in computer engineering.

**EDUCATION:**
In progress: BS, Computer Engineering • CSU Sacramento • GPA 3.65 • May 2013

**COURSES:**
Advanced Computer Organization Computer Interfacing CMOS and VLSI*
Advanced Logic Design Computer Network and Internet Electronic Materials
Computer Hardware Design Computer Software Engineering Network Analysis

**PROJECT EXPERIENCE:**
*Senior Project Design* – Automated Prescription Monitoring System:
Member of a four-person team that is developing an automated pill-dispensing machine with a portable pill case. An Arduino is embedded in both the dispenser and pill case. The pill case provides reminders to the patient and monitors slots being opened and closed. The collected data is uploaded to a MySQL database that stores data for each patient using the dispenser. A PHP website provides the user with the ability to edit prescription data and settings. An Android smartphone application is also being developed to provide reminders and prescription data.

*16-bit MIPS Processor:* Led a two-person team through the design, development and implementation phases of a 16-bit MIPS processor with a 5-stage pipeline. Behavioral modeling in Verilog was used to implement load/store word operations, integer arithmetic, and branching. Simple branch prediction, forwarding and hazard detection were also implemented.

*Cache/PCI Bus:* Led a two-person team through the design, development and implementation phases of a 4 KB, fully associative cache, capable of working between a PCI device and main memory to provide faster access to data. The entire simulation used PCI bus protocol to perform single reads and writes between the device and main memory.

**KNOWLEDGE AND SKILLS:**
Programming Languages: C • C++ • C# • Java • Verilog • VHDL • HTML • PHP • MySQL • x86 Assembly Operating Systems: Windows XP • Windows 7 • Unix • Linux Software: Visual Studio • Eclipse • ModelSim • Multisim • Matlab • Xilinx ISE • MS OfficeTools: Oscilloscope • Function Generator • Logic Analyzer

*Organizational and Communication Skills:*
• Strong analytical and problem-solving skills acquired through the completion of hardware and software projects
• Excellent written and oral communication skills developed through lab reports and group presentations.
• Highly organized having managed multiple projects simultaneously.
• Self-motivated and dependable; always complete projects before deadlines.

**WORK EXPERIENCE:**
Computer/Algebra Tutor Self-Employed Summers 2008 to 2012
Hardware Troubleshooter Self-Employed 7/09 – 8/09

**ACCOMPLISHMENTS AND ACTIVITIES:**
• Dean's Honor List
• Recipient, Henry T. Roche Scholarship and computer labs.

# ROBERT D. MCADAMS

200 Sesame Street. Elk Grove, CA 95604 • 916-123-4567 • rmcadams@email.com

**OBJECTIVE:** A position in software development involving computer or network security.

## EDUCATION
Bachelor of Science, Computer Science • CSU, Sacramento • Major GPA 3.1 • December 2013

## RELATED COURSES:
Computer System Attacks and Countermeasures Database Management Systems
Computer Forensics Principles and Practices Database Management and File Organization
Computer Software Engineering Intro to Systems Programming in UNIX
Computer Networks and Internets Object-Oriented Computer Graphics Programming

## KNOWLEDGE AND SKILLS
*Programming Languages:* ASP.NET, Perl, PHP, XML/RSS, (X/S/D)HTML, CSS, Javascript, SQL: Oracle/MySQL/SQLServer, Unix Shell Scripting, Java, Visual Basic, C/C++, Networking, Design/Specification/Quality Assurance Standards & Procedures
*Software Applications:* All MS Office applications, MS SharePoint, Open Office, Telnet, Remote Desktop, Cisco VPNs, Secure Shell, FTP, SFTP, Apache, all forms of Linux, Adobe: Acrobat 9 Pro, Premiere Elements 7/8, Photoshop Elements 7/8, JASC Paint Shop Pro 8, Kremlin/Bestcrypt/Truecrypt cryptology, Ad-Aware/Spybot security, ZoneAlarm/PC Tools/Windows firewalls
*Communications/Organization:*
Extremely fluent in English language, excellent business writing experience
Four years of High School Spanish, Independent study of Japanese
Experienced: public speaker, group/team leader, group/team member, individual worker

## PROJECT EXPERIENCE
*Senior Project*: As the team leader for a four person software web design project, directed and managed the creation of a new internet website for the CA Dept. of Public Health using ASP.NET and MS SharePoint to distribute and manage the system. This one-year project encompassed the entire software development life cycle including requirements and specifications, proposal development, customer consultation, software design, testing, development of user and maintenance manuals and delivery of a comprehensive user report and final presentation.

*Network Token Ring Design Project:* Implemented a messaging system in C++ utilizing "token ring" design structure. Established a 3 computer network using RS-232. Sent and received messages using TCP/IP and implemented CRC checksum error handling.

*Software Design Project:* Designed and implemented a system for the CSUS Psychology Department for data archival and retrieval. The system provided dynamic data storage and analysis for faculty, students, and community 3rd parties.

## WORK EXPERIENCE:
*Student Programmer California Energy Commission 7/07-12/09*
Converted legacy spreadsheet "database" for approved test labs to a relational database using MS Access. Additionally, I have created front-end input forms to allow for data control and to allow non-technical users to use the system. I have fully documented the database code, and created both user and admin/technical manuals.

*Contract Programmer NeTV 10/03-6/07*
Programmer and website security analyst for multiple clients and websites. Duties included server maintenance and security, as well as working with the FBI to trace spammers and cyber-criminals. Served as project leader coordinating design and client interactions on multiple occasions.

**9.2**

# PORTFOLIO CONSTRUCTION: A PRESENTATION TOOL FOR ADVANCED SERIOUS JOB SEEKING

A Portfolio is a hinged cover or flexible case for carrying loose papers, pictures or pamphlets. For job seeking and interviewing purpose it is a set of work samples, such as reports, drawings or photographs, either bound in book form or loose in a folder. **Portfolios are a tool commonly used by artists, architects, and interior designers to show potential clients and employers their work.**

*For all other professionals, it is a relatively new idea.* A portfolio is a way to show an employer samples of your work and pictures of projects you have worked on. It allows you to assemble, in an orderly fashion, representations of your best quality work. It gives you a chance to stand out from the competition by showing the employer you hope will hire you, a visual display of your work. You will most likely be sharing it in an interview.

*It is important to understand that a portfolio is not a resume.* A resume is a summary of your background and talents. A portfolio is a display of your work. (A resume should be included as the first item in your portfolio.)

Items that you choose to include in your portfolio depend in large part on what you have to show, and what you determine the employer needs to see. You will decide what to include after you have done some research and analysis. Read the job description and talk to people that currently work for the company to see what to emphasize. Visit the employer's web site to glean relevant information.

The employer is looking for a basic set of skills and some specialized expertise specific to their industry. **Included in the skills and expertise sought by employers are the following:**

> Technical Expertise
> Computer Skills
> Communications Skills:
> *written, verbal, presentation*
> Analytical/Problem Solving Skills:
> Leadership Skills
> Organization Skills
> Team Skills

*You should already know what skills you want to emphasize from the work we did with the Skills Assessment activities.*

For your portfolio, you want to be able to actually find and show the work you've produced that demonstrate these skills and expertise. Examples of your talents can be seen in the things you have done such as reports, projects, designs, drawings, computer programs, diagrams, flowcharts, class lists, documentation, memos, events, and letters of recommendations (employers are also looking for what others have said about you), etc.

They come from your:

> School work
> Work situations
> Professional activities
> Leisure activities
> Community activities

If you are a recent graduate your school projects (such as a senior project or your masters thesis project) will provide a rich sources of material to include in your portfolio.

If you are an experienced professional, your work product will be the source of materials for your portfolio.

To construct your portfolio you will need to get fresh, crisp, clean copies of the documents you plan to use. Do not use originals. Be sure to run spell checks on everything. And go to a professional copy service. Take pictures of your senior project with the whole team smiling! Then use the copies with captions under the pictures. You can get color copies at any of the commercial copy centers.

You will have to invest some money in stationary supplies such as sheet protectors, binders and dividers. Don't be cheap! Buy high quality supplies.

Your portfolio should not be just thrown together. It should be extremely well organized and very professional looking. You will need a table of contents at the beginning and you will need to place dividers with labels in front of each new item. You should not throw in absolutely everything; just use the most impressive representations of your work and skills.

Your table of contents might include:

> Resume
> References and Recommendation Letters
> Projects
> Writing Samples
> Photos

The use of a portfolio can really make you stand-out. It increases your confidence and it impresses employers. A portfolio helps you compete when the competition might have more experience. You will have a better presentation of your experience! That can make the difference in getting the job.

## 9.3

# ONLY YAHOOS LIE ON THEIR RESUMES

Lying on your resume is a disaster waiting to happen. On May 13, 2012, it was all over the news: Yahoo CEO, Scott Thompson, was fired for lying on his resume, claiming he had a degree in computer science. He has a degree in accounting and that should have been good enough, but he embellished his resume when he applied to Yahoo and claimed to have slightly better credentials than he actually has.

This is a very public shaming for a very public person. He shamed himself and he shamed Yahoo. He should have told the truth and Yahoo should have looked him up on Google and they should have carefully verified all of his professional and academic claims. He was applying for CEO for heavens sake!

Thompson spent just four months as CEO of Yahoo and will probably never have a job that good again. He may be able to parlay this fiasco into a book and a trip to the Oprah Show... Oh, but wait, the Oprah Show is gone and no one can find her on her new network...

If Thompson is smart, he may figure out how to reinvent himself. If not, he will spiral down into oblivion. He may get to spend some time at a federal prison too. He lied on his resume and he lied on a bio for an SEC filing. That is unforgivable.

American corporations are in no mood to tolerate lying or indiscretions of any kind. They are under the microscopes of the SEC, their shareholders, and the press. The SEC is now looking into Thompson and the Yahoo share price dropped on the news. HP CEO, Mark Hurd was fired for sexually harassing an underling. Best Buy CEO, Brian Dunn was fired for an inappropriate relationship with a female employee. JP Morgan's CIO, Ina Drew was fired for engaging in highly risky investing - the likes of which drove the recession that lasted for four long years. Where do these people come from?

According to a former Yahoo manager (who did not wish to be named): "Trust is one of the most important assets an individual has. Trust is earned. It is essential to professional success. When people lie, it destroys trust. Trust goes to the core values of honesty and integrity. Once the trust is betrayed, your career will be on a downward spiral. No one will ally with someone who is not trustworthy."

Lying always has its consequences. In the age of Google, lying will catch up with you.

Harvard student, Adam Wheeler, was arrested and charged with larceny and identity fraud after he lied on his Harvard application and on his resume, claiming that he authored several books among other things. He plead guilty to all 20 counts against him and was required to make restitution to Harvard for the grants he was awarded.

MIT Dean of Admission, Marilee Jones, was fired after 28 years for lying on her resume. She didn't earn the degrees that she claimed on her resume. Someone finally checked.

People frequently get caught because they make enemies in the workplace. It is usually about politics, money, or competition. That's what happened to the Yahoo CEO. A large stockholder had an issue, and there was a struggle for power and control. People with issues tend to do research.

Other times people get caught because their skills and talents don't match the demands of the job. One of the famous "Peter Principles" is that managers tend to "rise to their own level of incompetence." With a phony resume, sometimes they rise well beyond their "incompetence."

FEMA Director, Michael "heck-of-a-job-Brownie" Brown, contributed to the national disgrace of Hurricane Katrina. Brown lied on his resume, claiming that he managed emergency services for a city in Oklahoma and that he was a professor at a university that had never heard of him. If he had been honest when he applied for the job, the FEMA Director chosen would probably have been someone who knew what to do when the City of New Orleans was drowning.

How can people get away with this for so many years? It is not hard to understand. If you are moving up or across organizations, people assume that you were vetted properly before your last move. Some information is hard to verify, and if there is no reason to suspect something is wrong, who is going to go digging? Yahoo assumed that PayPal had vetted Scott Thompson when they hired him to be president of the company... Oops...

People who are willing to lie to get ahead are going to have good "impression management" skills. They are good talkers, like Leonardo DiCaprio's character in the movie "Catch Me If You Can". He was an impostor who knew how to talk his way out of a tight spot.

We like to think that successful candidates are vetted and tested before they are hired. What we learned from the Yahoo debacle is that the best person doesn't always win. When the liar is hired, they are denying all of the other more qualified candidates their rightful opportunity.

If you lie because you are ambitious and want to get ahead, your ambition will put you in competition with others sooner or later, and someone will figure it out, especially if you are nasty to people on the way up.

If you lie to cover up some problem in the past, it will come up the first time you make an enemy or some big mistake. If you screw up somehow, it is a lot easier to get rid of you if there is some lie you told just waiting to be uncovered.

People make mistakes in life or have career set-backs all of the time. We actually learn more from our failures than we learn from our successes.

The only way to successfully move forward is to emphasize your strengths and to be honest about your past. You do not have to advertise your flaws or failings, but you do not want to engage in a cover-up.

Build your resume on the solid ground of your accomplishments. Just tell the truth and you'll do fine.

# INTERVIEWS

## 10.0

# INTERVIEWS - THE ESSENTIALS OF YOUR PRESENTATION - PART 2

Interviewing effectively is an acquired skill. Very few people are so talented that they can do it well the first time without much preparation. If you really want to be successful in interviewing, I recommend that you start by understanding that there are things you must do before you interview, there are things to expect during an interview, as well as things you must do to follow up after an interview.

Employers are interested in some very specific things. They want to know that you fit their needs on a variety of things. They want to know that you have the right stuff. *The things that will either make or break your interview include:*

**01.** Do you have the technical expertise or breadth of knowledge necessary to perform the job? They will most definitely quiz you on your knowledge that fit with the needs of the position you are interviewing for.

**02.** Do you have solid communication skills? Can you communicate effectively with customers, clients, co-workers, other managers and the myriad of government agencies or subcontractors and organizations that interface with their company?

**03.** Do you have good computer skills? Can you create effective, professional documents?

*Bottom line, can you do the job?*

## 10.1

# WHAT TO DO BEFORE YOU START INTERVIEWING

**RESEARCH YOURSELF AND THE EMPLOYER** - Know yourself thoroughly: your goals, your interests, your values, your strengths and your weaknesses. Employers will be asking you questions on all of these topics to see how well you fit with the position for which they are hiring. Take time and write out lists. Start by listing your long-term and your short-term goals. Where do you want to be in 3 to 5 years? Where do you want to be in 7 to 10 years? What are your interests? What knowledge do you have that you really want to apply?

What are your greatest strengths? What are some of your weaknesses, and what are you doing to improve?

Know the employer thoroughly before your interview. Research as much as possible through the web and by visiting the job site and meeting with current employees to gather information about the available positions. You will want to know as much as you can about what specific expertise you will be using so you can go back and study notes from past classes and read current articles on industry related topics. You will want to study as if you are preparing for a final exam. Successful candidates have told me that they spend about 6 hours studying before an interview.

Now put together what you know about yourself and what you have learned about the employer and figure out how you fit the needs of the position and the organization.

You will be asked questions like "Why are you interested in this position?" and "Why do you believe you would be successful in this position?"

Interviews are not really a mystery if you understand that employers are looking for a candidate that fits with their organization. They are going to ask you some standard questions. After a few interviews, you will quickly discover that they all ask pretty much the same questions. You can prepare for standard questions by reading a book that I recommend called "Knock 'em Dead" by Martin Yate. It has a great list of questions, and it includes some really good answers so you can see what makes for a good answer.

## WHAT HAPPENS DURING THE INTERVIEW

**RELAX** - Interviews are just like any conversation with a new person. Employers will size you up based on how relaxed you are, if you are dressed professionally, if you know how to shake hands and just how well you handle meeting new people for the first time. Little things like showing up a little early, smiling, being confident and being extremely well prepared make all the difference in the world. I recommend that you show up at least 20 minutes early to use the restroom, do breathing exercises and review your notes, your resume, and your portfolio before your interview.

You can expect that you may be interviewed by several people over the course of the day, so don't double schedule yourself. Share all information with enthusiasm with each person even if you end up saying the same thing seven or eight times.

My absolute best recommendation is to walk into every interview with the following thought on your mind... "If this job doesn't come through, something better will." That gives you confidence even when you have been interviewing for three months and you are just about panicked that you will never get a job. I promise you that you will get a job... Chances are that if you are reading this book you don't qualify to be permanently unemployed! It is just going to require that you find the right company and be extremely well prepared. It will happen.

## WHAT TO DO AFTER AN INTERVIEW

**DEBRIEF AND FOLLOW UP** - After an interview you will want to sit in your car and scream or disintegrate into a little puddle. Resist the urge... Instead immediately write down everything you remember about the interview. This will help you prepare for your next interview by allowing you to analyze your performance and do better in your next interview or salvage the interview with a plan. What questions were you asked? What did you do well? What did you do poorly? What do you wish you had done or said that you did not?

Next, send a thank you note to each of the persons who interviewed you. Thank them for the time they spent interviewing you and tell them that you appreciated the opportunity to share your interests and career goals. Tell them that you would welcome an opportunity to work in their company and tell them why. If you feel you could have answered a question more effectively, tell them what your answer would be now that you have had time to think. Many people that I have helped over the years have told me that sending a thank you note was the thing that distinguished them from the other candidates and got them the job.

Always follow up after an interview with a phone call in 2 to 3 days. Tell them that you are "checking on the status of your application"

## 10.2    TYPICAL QUESTIONS ASKED DURING INTERVIEWS

Why are you interested in our company?

What do you know about our company?

What makes you qualified for this position?

What are your long-term goals (i.e. what do you want to accomplish in the next 5-7 years)?

What are your short-term goals (i.e. what do you want to accomplish in the next 3-5 years)?

What are your greatest strengths?  What are your weaknesses?

How would you describe the ideal boss?

What tools do you believe you will need to be successful in your career?

What courses did you enjoy the most during your education? Why?

What courses did you like the least? Why?

What courses gave you the most difficulty? Why?

Describe your senior/masters project.

What was the most challenging aspect of your senior/masters project?

What conflicts arose during the course of your project? How did you resolve the conflicts?

How would the members of your team describe you?

Describe any leadership roles you have had during the past 4 years.

**Do you prefer to work in teams or alone?**

Describe your related work experience. What did you learn? Why was it important?

What is communication and why is it important to your success in a company?

Do you have anything to add?  Do you have any questions?

and that you are very interested in the job. One employer told me that he waited for candidates to follow up with a phone call and did not hire anyone who did not call.

## 10.3

# QUICK GUIDE TO PHASES OF A SUCCESSFUL JOB INTERVIEW

### BREAKING THE ICE PHASE

Arrive 30 minutes early! Relax and tell yourself "if this job doesn't come through, something better will". When called for your interview, start with a warm, firm handshake and a smile as you introduce yourself. Maintain eye contact when speaking to your host/interviewer. This is a formal interview so don't be too casual or familiar with the people you meet. Be polite and courteous. Ask for a business card to help you remember their name and functional area.

### SHARING GENERAL INFORMATION PHASE

Once you are seated your interview will begin with broad open-ended questions like "Tell me about yourself"; "Why did you choose this field?"; "Why are you interested in our company?"; "Why are you interested in this position?"; "What courses did you enjoy the most?"; "What are your long term/short term goals?"; "Tell me about your work experience." They will also ask personality trait questions like "What is your greatest strength?" and behavioral questions like "Give an example of

how you used this strength to solve a problem in a team project?"; "What is your greatest accomplishment and why?". Show them your portfolio during this stage if you can work it into an answer.

### TECHNICAL QUESTIONS PHASE

This phase is like a final exam. The technical questions you will be asked will stretch your technical expertise to the limit. Be prepared to cover material that relates to the company's mission, products and industry. This is where your research and course review will pay off. Be prepared to be intensely questioned on the field-specific courses you have taken and anything you have listed on your resume. Spending 6 hours studying before the interview is standard.

### INTERVIEWING THE INTERVIEWER PHASE

This is your opportunity to shine. If you have done your homework you will be able to ask good questions about the company's position in the industry, training programs, initial project that new college grads work on and anything you can glean from headlines or professional journals. A successful candidate with an energy regulatory agency asked questions about a current crisis that was in the news and featured in technical journals. The interviewers were very impressed.

### SUMMARY PHASE

At this point the interviewer will ask, "Do you have anything to add?" You will want to think back over what you have included thus far and add anything you have not covered yet. It is also your opportunity to summarize your most important points (senior project, pertinent work experience and class experience. Make sure you pop out your portfolio if you have not already done so).

## WRAP UP AND WHAT'S NEXT PHASE

This is your last shot. Tell them you really want the job. Ask about further steps you should take (completing an application form, sending transcripts, sharing references).

Also ask when you can expect to hear from them. Ask for a business card if you have not already gotten one. When leaving shake hands, and thank them for the interview with a big smile. Tape the business card into your notebook and debrief. Then send an email thank you note immediately!

# 10.4

# ASKING THE INTERVIEWER QUESTIONS GETS THE JOB!

Candidates often ask me how to prepare for a job interview. One often-overlooked element of preparation is developing a list of questions you can ask the interviewer. Candidates should have a few well-researched questions ready to ask the interviewer when it gets to that often-awkward "Now, do you have any questions for me?" part of the interview. Employers are always impressed when someone has something really intelligent to ask at that point (something that shows not only that they are interested, but also that they know enough about what the company does to be able to craft a good question).

Every now and then I work with someone who is clueless about their impact on others. This is particularly lethal in an interview situation. I once had reason to call an interviewer at Lawrence Livermore National Labs to find out what one of my students had done wrong in the interview. The student asked me how he could improve his interview skills, since he had received a call indicating that he had been rejected after the interview. He needed feedback from the interviewer. He really felt he had done well in the interview. He thought he had been right on with his answers and that an offer would be forthcoming. I made a call to the interviewer to get some frank information about how the interview had gone. There were a series of small mistakes (things that might have been overlooked for a geek candidate) - somewhat sloppy appearance, a bit of awkwardness but the biggest complaint from the interviewer was that the candidate didn't have any questions when it came to that stage of the interview. Very bad!

Asking questions demonstrates enthusiasm. You need to have questions to ask! It looks like you didn't do your homework or that you are not really interested in the position or the company if you don't have any questions. You have to have a question or two for each and every person who interviews you. In many instances, multiple people will interview you during a visit to a company that is considering you for employment. You can ask the same questions throughout the day to get different people's opinions. Human resources people will interview you early in the process. But as you make your way through the day, you will be interviewed by people you will work with and people you will work for. The manager frequently interviews you last.

When I discussed the feedback I had received with the candidate, he said he had asked questions of almost everyone, but that by the end of the day he felt he had enough information and that he just stopped asking questions of the last person or two. He was also tired. Well that didn't work too well did it? The last interviewers of the day frequently have the most influence. They are frequently the people who are the most powerful. They are also the people who remember best what occurred in the interview because the information is fresh in their minds. They are the last people to speak with you before they meet to decide whether you should be hired or not... And there you are, too tired and too worn out to make a good impression. Really!

Wake up! Make sure you are making a good impression on everyone you talk to throughout the entire interview process. Everyone you meet is important. Everyone who interviews you will weigh in on the decision. Answer the questions of the last interviewer with as much gusto as you showed the first person that interviewed you. If you feel yourself fatiguing during the interview day, hit the bathroom and throw cold water on your face. Say to yourself, "This is it! This is where all of that hard work pays off! I cannot afford to let up now! I have to be fresh and energized. I don't qualify to be permanently unemployed."

You are like a runner, a swimmer or an Olympic athlete. You have to reach way down within yourself and find that inner strength to do your best for a longer period than you thought possible. You can do it! I know you can! You will be glad you did.

## 10.5

# PHONE INTERVIEWS DONE RIGHT!

Many people struggle with what to do when confronted with an interview on the telephone. Telephone interviews are one of the toughest events a job seeker faces. First of all, the phone call frequently comes unexpectedly or at an inconvenient time. Secondly, you have more difficulty judging the reaction to your comments and answers when you cannot see a person's face. Should you continue? Should you stop? Hard to say. Thirdly, it is harder to establish rapport with someone when you are not in the same room. There are things you can do to make yourself more comfortable and improve your chances of a positive outcome with a telephone interview.

The first rule of telephone interviewing is: *get information before giving information.*

Ask for the name and title of the person calling and what department they are calling from. You will also want to ask what position they will be interviewing you for. I would also suggest that you ask them to describe to you the available position or positions. You will also need the phone number of the person so that if you get disconnected you will be able to call them back. (If you are on your cell phone, it should capture the number but if the number is blocked you may not get the number if you do not ask for it, so always ask).

Rule number two of telephone interviewing is: do not allow yourself to go through an interview if you feel you are not at your very best. It is OK to ask to schedule another time when you are more prepared. Your chances of making a good impression are much better if you are feeling good when you are interviewed. You will want to reschedule for the soonest possible time. Sometimes you may just want to get your thoughts and notes together. You can ask if you can call them back in ten to fifteen minutes.

Picture this. You just got home from a long day of work or if you are a student from classes and working on your senior project. It is 9 PM and you are rung out, dead tired and you haven't had anything to eat since early morning. The phone rings and it turns out to be a manager from a company you met at a job fair. (Since some candidates are hard to reach during the day, managers frequently call late at night to try to catch you). How do you handle it? Do you really want to be interviewed under these circumstances? It is a great company and you would just love to work for them but you don't want to blow it by answering tough questions while you are in a hunger fog. Since you are not at your best, you want to reschedule the phone interview to a time when you can put your best foot forward.

If the call came at a time when you are not too tired or distracted or stressed or disorganized or dripping on the rug because you just stepped out of the shower, the time you spend listening to the information the caller/employer is sharing with you will allow you to get your thoughts and notes together so that when the questions begin, you will know who you are interviewing with and what position you are being interviewed for. You will know what you want to say about your background because you will have information on which to base your comments.

If you are too tired or have had a beer and don't feel you can present well, ask if you can schedule a time when you are fresher and more alert. Get a phone number and an email address. Be sure to establish who is calling whom at the appointed time. Then email a confirmation and tell them you are looking forward to your phone interview. Make sure when you are being interviewed that you find a quiet place and pull yourself together and assemble your notes before the call.

Sometimes it is best to just not answer. Yes, you can just ignore the phone when you might make a less than favorable impression. That is why you pay for a voice message service. Use it!

Remember the career binder with the A to Z index, that you developed to organize your career plan, where you file all of the information on the jobs you are applying for by company name? Now is when it will pay off. Be sure to place the binder by the phone for easy access when the phone call comes in. Have fresh paper and a pen in the binder to take notes while the caller is explaining the available position and giving you his/her contact information. Review anything you have from your previous contacts with the company: review job descriptions; information gathered during your research on the company; the history of your application process including names of the individuals to whom you have sent your resume.

Telephone interviews can work out great! Just make sure you are at your best and that you have everything you need at your fingertips when you go through one.

## 10.6

# INTERVIEW AND DINING ETIQUETTE: YOU ARE BEING JUDGED

A meal, dinner, lunch or even breakfast might easily be the first stage of your interview. You will need to traverse a minefield of dining mistakes that could cost you the job. Even after you get the job, you will profit or suffer because of your manners. Good manners are always in style. Never forget that!

In life it's the little things that matter, the little things that make an impression: a smile, a door held open, a thank you note, and nice table manners. These are the things that get noticed and that make you stand out. Or maybe it is the absence of the little things that make an impression. Good manners mean that you have good judgment. That is really important to potential employers.

One candidate that I worked with could have used some help on his table manners. He clearly forgot everything his mother told him. He flew all the way to Detroit, Michigan to interview for a job with GM (at their expense!). His interview started with breakfast at 7 AM along with a group of other new grad candidates from across the country. By 7:30 AM he had blown the entire interview. How could that be? He ordered steak and eggs... because it was on the menu... and he could. (He was thrilled to be able to order such a treat, forgetting that the job interview was the big event he was in Detroit for).

Then, when confronted with a dull knife, he proceeded to fork the steak and lift the entire thing to his mouth. (It was a small little steak, he told me later). As he opened his mouth to take a bite, he looked up and saw the entire assemblage around the table open their mouths and stare in horror. He knew immediately it was over. Needless to say, no offer came at the end of the day.

My daughter was recently in a position to give input on who was hired to replace her when she left her internship. Each person let down their guard when they were in the room alone with her after the interview to ask questions, not knowing she would be sharing her impressions of candidates with the employer.

The lesson is treat everyone you meet on site at the interview as though they will be part of the decision!

Sometimes when people are nervous they forget the most obvious little things. Good manners are basic common sense. Sometimes we get out of the habit of using our best manners. But manners are essential to your success in life. They are the lubricant that make

social interactions run smoothly. The absence of good manners can make an otherwise good situation turn sour.

## 10.7

# COSTLY ERRORS THAT KILL JOB OFFERS

Over the years, I have had an opportunity to observe many people during their job searches. Most people are pretty careful about how they present themselves, but there are some glaring errors that have been deal breakers for even the most talented candidates I have worked with. The owner of a small engineering firm in Auburn called me, after posting a position on the web, to say that he had selected the candidates that he would be interviewing. He was astounded that he had received a number of cover letters that were so poorly written that he will not even consider interviewing the candidates who sent them.

*Having errors in your cover letter or on your resume will instantly turn the employer off.* The resume and cover letter review is the first screening that an employer does of the potential candidate. Why should they waste any time on someone who cannot get it together on paper? I worked with one job seeker who came to me wondering why he was not having any luck getting an interview. After looking at his resume for about five seconds I noticed he had Microsoft spelled wrong... NEVER SEND ANYTHING WITHOUT PROOF-READING IT or having someone else proof your work. Often times, we miss our own errors because we see what we expect to see, so solicit the help of someone who writes well.

***Stumbling into an interview late is just plain rude and is not going to win you a job.*** Always plan for unexpected delays and build plenty of time into your schedule. Plan to arrive at your interview thirty minutes to an hour early. Even if there was a traffic jam, it is a lame excuse to present to an employer you have kept waiting. And if the employer is interviewing multiple people on a tight schedule, your interview will be cut short.

***Arriving for an interview unprepared is a major mistake.*** It shows a distinct lack of interest in the job and a basic disrespect for the person interviewing you. Average preparation time for a successful interview is about six hours. Figure you are studying for the ultimate final, the one that makes all of that education pay off. What is involved? Well you need to know yourself thoroughly: list your goals, your greatest strengths, your interests, your related work experience. Do an inventory of who you are.

Then do some research on the company. Figure out what technical information you need to study. Study old notes from past training and classes, and find current articles on the company and the industry. Then, put it all together. Why are you qualified for the position and what do you need to share about yourself in the interview to get the job? Assemble a portfolio of your work to share with the interviewer. Hewlett Packard, or example, expects to see samples of your work from your senior project or other significant projects you have worked on.

***Rambling on in the interview about irrelevant information is a waste of the interviewer's time.*** I once worked with a candidate who had just finished his Masters degree. He was getting interviews but he was not getting any job offers at a time when everyone else was landing the jobs they wanted. I had him come to my office prepared to be interviewed. He came in dressed in his suit, with his resume and his portfolio, and a list of questions he was being asked. I proceeded to interview him. I started our mock interview with "Tell me about yourself." He responded that he had grown up on a farm in Patterson, and his performance went downhill from there. He spoke about his farm and his dog. That is not what the employer wants to hear. The employer wants you to tell him/her who you are relative to the job you are interviewing for. He started again and told me that he had built his first computer in a 4H club and that this experience had propelled him toward his engineering degree and a focus on electronic engineering and computer architecture.

***Failure to maintain good grooming and personal appearance.*** A sloppy appearance in an interview indicates to the employer that you are careless and unprofessional. It is absolutely required that you have a professional looking interview outfit and that you maintain it by having it dry cleaned regularly.

***Failure to maintain a positive attitude.*** This is perhaps the hardest one to remember after you have been rejected by multiple employers.

It takes three to six months minimum to find a job. Looking for a job is a full time job! You will have to devote all of your efforts to the goal of getting a job if you expect to get results. You will have to be utterly positive for the entire search. If you walk into an interview with a dejected look, you have blown the interview before you even open your mouth. You must truly believe that you do not qualify to be permanently unemployed and that the perfect job will come along. It will help if you burn off stress with some serious exercise plan that you execute each and every day. And each and every time you walk into an interview, you must say to yourself: "If this job doesn't come through, something better will." And you must believe it!

Sweat the details and get help if you need it!

10.8

# SLOBS DON'T GET JOBS!

Far too often I notice people showing up to job fairs and interviews with a laid-back attitude and looking pretty casual. As a matter of fact, some candidates are in slinky party outfits or worse, jeans and t-shirts. Many do not bring a portfolio of their work or even a resume. This is just not acceptable! These are formal hiring opportunities. Some will justify this with a shrug - that the clothes they choose reflect who they are. Well, that attitude is likely to result in unemployment. Slobs don't get jobs!

*Job Fairs and formal interviews require a professional presentation of yourself and of your credentials.* You only get one chance to make a good first impression. First professional impressions are usually made at job fairs, in interviews, or at professional conferences and conventions. You need to look good! You need to look like a serious professional both in your attire an in your job seeking documents. If you do not, you will not get hired. It is as simple as that. There are way too many highly qualified people on the market for you to look like a dip and expect to get a job.

*It is going to cost you a bit to get your fashion act together, but it is totally worth it.* Great places to shop include:

- Men's Warehouse (men only)
- Talbot's (women only)
- Nordstrom's (if you have unlimited resources)
- Macy's, JCPenney, and Kohl's (if you have modest resources)
- Landsend.com (if you hate shopping)
- J Crew and Banana Republic (if you love shopping)
- Gap (slacks for the business casual look)
- Thrift stores (if you have no money and unlimited time)

These are all places where you can find the professional outfit you are looking for. And an added bonus at the end of the season is that everything was on big discount sale! I helped my daughter Elizabeth find (and buy) an interview outfit at Banana Republic and things were 75% off- really nice stuff!

I know you have no time to accomplish this task now. You need a nice professional outfit anyway. As a matter of fact, everyone does. This doesn't have to be painful or take a long time. Just before a career event one year I stopped at Talbot's and picked up a new jacket and top. I just walked in, told the clerk what I wanted and I walked out 15 minutes later with a skirt that is one size smaller than I thought I needed. Well, that was a treat!!! And the items were more than 60% off!

*First, inventory your wardrobe.* If you open the closet and all you see are t-shirts and jeans, you know you have your work cut out for you. No, khaki pants are not formal professional attire. I know, I know. Everyone at the companies you want to work for wears them just about everyday. But we are not talking about everyday wear for after you have the job, we are talking about what you will wear while trying to get the job.

*Next, make a list of items for your shopping spree.* Here are items you need to purchase: A suit or slacks/skirt/dress and a nice complimentary color blazer/jacket; multiple long sleeve white or light blue shirts/blouses; 2-3 neck ties (men) (buy the extras for when you drip spaghetti on your tie); A belt (men); and matching shoes.

*Buy only natural fiber items*
- *Shirts should be wrinkle resistant cotton*
- *Blouses can be silk or cotton*
- *Slacks should be made of worsted wool or gabardine.*
- *These fabrics breath and are good for summer as well as winter*
- *No polyester!!!*
- *Avoid linen - it wrinkles*

**Go conservative. Reminders to help you avoid interaction with the fashion police:**

• *Navy blue, grey, black and sometimes olive green are good color choices for slacks and skirts or suits. These colors never go out of style*
• *No colored or printed t-shirts under your shirt, they show through*
• *Don't show skin that should be covered*
• *No white socks*
• *Don't wear excessive jewelry - keep it simple*
• *Avoid perfume or cologne*
• *Hide your tattoos*

*Having your wardrobe together will make a huge difference in projecting a professional image to the employers you hope will employ you.*
Impress them once and you are in the door. Startle them or surprise them with your wardrobe, and that may be all they think about while speaking with you.

You feel better when you look good too... and that is the point. You need to feel good and you need to project a good image.


## 10.9


# YOUTHFUL INDISCRETIONS


Everyone has skeletons in their closet. Things that you have done that you wish you had not. Sometimes it is something small that just goes into long-term memory as a learning experience. Other times it is something that will come back to haunt you. Cleaning out the closet is not always an easy task but it is entirely necessary before you start applying for career level positions.

Over the years, I have worked with numerous individuals who have had stellar academic careers with amazing technical talent that got caught up in an unemployed purgatory. When they applied for jobs they found questions on applications that were tough to answer: Have you ever been convicted of a felony? Have you used drugs? Do you have a DUI conviction? Who knew at 18 that you might want a real job at 26?

Here is how it happens that your past catches up with you. When you least expect it – something that you totally forgot or suppressed in your memory - severely disrupts your employability. Unpaid debt, criminal history, drug use, a DUI all are things that can be dredged up by potential employers to be weighed in the employment decision.

The web has created all new searchable sources of information for investigators hired by your potential employer. Topics employers are forbidden to ask in an interview are exposed: Are you married? Are you engaged? Do you have a girl friend/boy friend? How old are you? Have you ever been sick? Have you ever been seriously injured? What is your religion? What is your nationality? Have you ever been arrested?

YouTube, Twitter, Facebook, and MySpace have given employers and investigators a wealth of information they would never have otherwise had. Things are frequently posted impulsively without thought for the future consequences. There it is – your dirty laundry – right out in public space – pictures of you sitting suggestively on someone's lap or guzzling beer at a tailgate party. It might not even be on your FB page... it could be on someone else's page and there you are – exposed for the entire world to see.

After an offer of employment is made, the background checks and lab tests begin. Expect to be subjected to drug tests, a DMV check, a credit report check, a criminal background check, and an extensive web search.

Troubleshooting problems after they cause you heart burn is way less desirable than identifying any and all potential issues before starting your job search. Once the application is in, and the offer is made, it is almost always too late to do damage control. The earlier things are corrected the better off you will be.

The people who do background checks are former FBI or law enforcement agents. Anything you have to hide, they will find. Whatever youthful indiscretion you engaged in will sound much worse when you are confronted with it by your now disillusioned prospective employer.

It sometimes takes a lot more than memory loss to repair the damage done by youthful indiscretions. Sometimes it is necessary to bring in an expert.

Over the 30+ years that I have been a career counselor, I have sorted out the aftermath of the disaster caused by little mistakes made before and during college for a number of individuals.

I once worked with someone, who at 18, had been caught on a convenience store video camera with a new "dorm friend," who unbeknownst to him, was using a stolen credit card. He was caught in the arrest sweep and charged with credit card theft and fraud. He did not want to tell his parents, thinking he could handle it on his own. When he applied for jobs at 26, he never dreamed that the misdemeanor he pleaded to would be dredged up after he was made an offer. The offer was instantly withdrawn and he came to me in desperation for damage control.

The most important lessons that this person learned include: choose your friends carefully, and tell your parents when you get into trouble. No one cares more about you than your parents. No one will bring more resources to bear than your parents will. They will move heaven and earth to help you out of a jam.

He also learned that the help of an expert makes a huge difference. You do not have to suffer. You do not have to be embarrassed. I have seen it all. Nothing shocks me.

The withdrawn offer was reinstated after a critical analysis of the situation and a well-written letter carefully explained this youthful indiscretion, as well as the significant accomplishments achieved in the ensuing eight years, and the lessons learned.

It is never easy to recover from something like this but it can be done. It is definitely best to sort it out with an expert before applying for career level positions.

## 10.10

# DOES THE HANDSHAKE MATTER?

©*Paul Mattiuzzi, PhD. Used with permission.*

*It's not just common sense. The research shows that the handshake matters. It does in fact contribute to "first impressions." It is not an entirely bogus way for people to judge you: your handshake actually reflects certain personality characteristics. And the research shows that when it comes to self-promotion, handshake etiquette may be more important for women than for men.*

*Everyone knows, from personal experience, that we make judgments about people based on how they shake hands. It's one thing to say "hi" or "good morning" to someone you pass on the street. It is something entirely different to engage someone at the level of touching hands and making physical contact. Sometimes it might mean nothing at all, like at a gathering where you are introduced to one person after the next. If you are* a politician, you might shake hundreds of hands in the course of just a few minutes, simply because people want to connect to you. But there are other times when this ritual of personal engagement is a prelude to more important business that will follow. It could be at the start of a contest or negotiation, or in advance of an important interview, or upon meeting the parents or the family. Handshakes are an important introductory ritual in all manner of social contacts, and the research shows that the quality of the handshake makes a real difference.

There have been a number of studies that explore the dynamics of handshaking, but the one that stands out is an article by University of Alabama psychologists William F. Chaplin et al published in 2000 in the Journal of Personality and Social Psychology.

What is unique about their study is that rather than gathering subjective data, they made an effort to provide objective measurements of the variables of interest. Their method itself is of interest.

The subjects in the study were introduced to four different "handshake judges" in a way that made it seem natural that they would be greeted with a handshake. Following the introduction, the subjects completed a set of personality tests, providing an independent measure of whether or not their handshakes reflected any actual personality differences.

Before being sent out to evaluate handshakes, the judges trained and practiced for a month, until they could reliably distinguish eight different handshake characteristics: completeness of grip, temperature, dryness, strength, duration, vigor, texture, and eye contact. In normal situations, it may not be the case that anyone actually judges you on all of these factors, but it is worth noting that these variables might all be in play when you do shake someone's hand. In addition to evaluating the characteristics of each handshake, the judges were asked their impressions about the personality characteristics displayed by each participant.

Although the judges rated the subjects on a full set of personality traits, it turned out that the handshake did not actually allow them to draw clear distinctions on particular traits. The judges did form consistent opinions of those whose hands they shook, but the judgments were global, rather than specific. They could reliably agree only on whether the handshake conveyed a "good impression" or a "poor impression."

It also turned out that the individual handshake characteristics (i.e., vigor, duration, eye-contact, etc.) were all highly correlated. In other words, people are not usually judged on these factors individually, and instead, the differences tend to collapse into one global factor which is best described as a "firm handshake."

After a month of training in how to judge a handshake, the judges were able to reliably identify those who had a firm handshake and to reliably distinguish those whose handshake provided for either a "good" or a "poor" impression.

As to how a "firm handshake" corresponded to the measured personality factors, what they found is that it does correlate with factors such as "openness to new experience" and extroversion. Those who did not have a "firm handshake" were found to score higher on measures of "neuroticism" (which means that they tend to be more prone to anxiety) and to display more "shyness." In other words, from your handshake, people can learn whether or not you are shy and anxious, and whether you are "open" and outgoing.

The key points here may seem obvious, but it is worth repeating: people do in fact form impressions based on the quality of your handshake, and those impressions do reflect certain elements of your personality.

As to how this relates to "first impressions," the authors' next finding is particularly interesting. Women with a firm handshake were viewed as more "open," and made a more favorable impression. It is sometimes thought that when women *present themselves as outgoing and confident, others will judge them negatively, believing that they are "pushy" or aggressive. What this research shows is that at least when it comes to the hand-shake, women benefit from appearing strong and are not penalized for appearing confident. For men, the effect was not as strong. In other words, a woman benefits more from having a firm hand-shake than does a man. For both genders, a weak handshake tends to generate less favorable impres-sions.*

*What this means is that everyone, both men and women, should pay attention to how they go about shaking hands. People are judging you and assessing your personality and character based on this moment of touch. For women, having a firm handshake is probably more important than for men.*

*The other point to be drawn from this study is that while your handshake is to some extent a genuine reflection of your actual personality, it can still be a practiced and developed skill. Think of the judges who spent a month learning how to receive a handshake and then realize that you can perfect and improve your own method before that important meeting.*

## 10.11

# POLISHING YOUR INTERVIEWING SKILLS: A WORD TO ESL CANDIDATES

Communication in an interview is about many things - among them - body language, clear speaking, and appropriate behavior. What you know is very important in interviewing but if the person interviewing you has diffi-culty understanding you or if you offend them unknowingly, you are not going to get the job.

Content, delivery, and form are all essential elements for interview success. Your resume, expertise, and company knowledge might get you an interview but it will not get you the job.

Your form matters as much as your content. You send your message with facial cues and body language. You will have to give good an-swers and deliver those answers effectively to get yourself hired. Fail in the delivery and you will be denied the opportunity to show the em-ployer just how good you are – how technically proficient you are.

Confidence plays a big part in delivering an-swers effectively. You will be meeting the peo-ple you hope will hire you for the first time and you must impress flawlessly. You want to be confident that you know the material and confident that you know proper protocol.

Over the years, I have worked with a number of individuals for whom English is their second language, frequently having moved to the United States as young adults.

Interviewing can be doubly stressful and much more challenging for the non-native born because the cultural norms for formal behavior differ from country to country.

This section is designed to help people for whom English is a second language interview more effec-tively. You will find practical strategies that will help you deliver optimal American English com-munication during interviews. We will discuss body language; rate, volume and intonation of speech; pronouncing English sounds and words correctly; and warm-up exercises for the best voice and pronunciation.

Dr. Celeste Roseberry-McKibbin, Professor of Speech Pathology and Audiology at CSU Sacra-mento, has generously given her permission for the use of her notes on how to improve commu-nication skills in interview situations. She has worked in educational and medical settings with a wide variety of clients.

Dr. Roseberry-McKibbin's primary research interests are in the areas of assessment and treatment of multicultural students with communication disorders as well as service delivery to children from low-income backgrounds. She has over 50 publications, including 6 books, and has made over 270 presentations at the local, state, national, and international levels. Dr. Roseberry-McKibbin is a Fellow of the American Speech-Language-Hearing Association, and won the Upton Sinclair Outstanding Educator Award for her service to children in poverty. She is a Fellow of the California Speech and Hearing Association, and received the American Speech-Language-Hearing Association's Certificate of Recognition for Contributions in Multicultural Affairs.

## 10.12

# PRACTICAL STRATEGIES FOR OPTIMAL ENGLISH COMMUNICATION DURING INTERVIEWS

*©Celeste Roseberry-McKibbin used with permission*

### BODY LANGUAGE

*Eye contact:* In many cultures, it is considered courteous to look down when one is speaking to an authority figure. However, in the United States, people greatly value direct eye contact. If you look down or away, people view you as not being confident or trustworthy. Therefore, direct and sustained eye contact is very important.

*Do not bow your head or look up through your*

eyelashes. Americans view this as submissive and indicative of a lack of confidence. If you need to think, look up--not down. Looking down makes you appear to lack confidence.

*Posture:* It is important to sit and stand as straight as possible. The straighter your posture, the more confidence you project. Relatedly, try not to cross your arms or legs. In the United States, this is viewed as being defensive and not open.

*Gestures:* It is acceptable to use a few facial or hand gestures but do not use too many. Using too many gestures makes you appear nervous.

Be sure to smile occasionally. Americans smile more than people from many other countries. If you never smile, American employers will think you are unfriendly and unapproachable.

### Rate, Volume, and Intonation of Speech
*Speed Rate:* It is extremely important to not speak too fast. The biggest mistake most people make during interviews is speaking too quickly. Interviews are stressful by nature and the inclination is try to finish an answer as soon as possible. Rapid speech makes you look nervous and less confident. It is best to speak slowly, and pause occasionally. This will make you appear more confident and more knowledgeable.

*Volume:* Another mistake made in interviews is speaking too softly. In some cultures, speaking softly is a sign of authority and power. In the U.S., speaking softly often means that you lack authority and lack confidence. Be sure to speak loudly enough.

Do not "trail off" at the end of sentences. Keep your volume or loudness at a good level until you have reached the end of your sentence.

*Intonation:* End sentences with a slightly downward inflection. If you end sentences with a slightly upward inflection, you sound hesitant and uncertain.

You also sound hesitant and uncertain if you use a number of qualifiers.

For example: "I think that, perhaps we might talk about this--I could be wrong, but..."

Let your intonation vary. If you speak in a

*monotone, people will think you are boring. People who speak with varied intonation patterns sound more interesting and intelligent.*

## PRONOUNCING ENGLISH SOUNDS AND WORDS CORRECTLY

*One pattern that is characteristic of many speakers of English as a foreign language is dropping the ending sounds off of words. This happens because in many languages, words end in vowels. In English, many words end in consonants and it is important to pronounce these consonants clearly. If you drop off the last consonant in the word, Americans will not understand you as well. Practicing can help you improve your pronunciation.*

### PRACTICE WORDS:

| | |
|---|---|
| *cat* | *pick* |
| *sheep* | *bus* |
| *glass* | *tape* |
| *goat* | *cab* |
| *dog* | *luck* |
| *bed* | *leaf* |
| *desk* | *heart* |
| *match* | *leg* |

*In some languages, words only contain one syllable. In English, many words are polysyllabic. It is important to pronounce all the syllables slowly and clearly. This will help you sound clearer when you speak.*

### PRACTICE WORDS:

| | |
|---|---|
| *elephant* | *olive* |
| *telephone* | *almost* |
| *interviewing* | *office* |
| *punctuality* | *opposite* |

*Stretch out your vowels. Many speakers of English as a foreign language "clip" or shorten their vowels. Americans have great difficulty understanding these speakers.*

## WARM-UP EXERCISES FOR THE BEST VOICE AND PRONUNCIATION

*When Americans speak, they open their mouths wider and move their lips more than speakers of many other languages do. It is a big adjustment for many speakers of English as a foreign language is to learn how to do this. It feels quite uncomfortable at first! But the more you open your mouth and move your lips when you are talking, the more easily Americans will understand you.*

*Additionally, if you speak with a tight jaw and very little lip movement you will make a bad impression because you will sound like you are mumbling. Speaking with an open and relaxed jaw, and good lip movement, makes you sound clear, relaxed, and authoritative.*

*Warm-up exercises can help. You can do these at home before your interview:*

*a. Yawn as wide as you can and say "yah." Do this 5-6 times.*
*b. Say "uuu-eee" as fast as you can 10-12 times.*
*c. Say "ma-may-mee-mo-mu" 5 times*
*d. Say "ta-tay-tee-to-tu" 5 times*
*e. Say "ka-kay-kee-ko-ku" 5 times Say the following words, opening your mouth as wide as possible on the first sound of each word.*

*Move your lips as much as you can when pronouncing each word:*

*opera*
*owl*
*always*
*hour*
*outside*
*awful*
*oddly*
*army*

### OTHER HELPFUL TIPS AND STRATEGIES

*Do not use interjections such as "um, you know." Employers react very negatively to this. Who sounds more confident and knowledgeable?*

*Weak delivery: "I um, I know that um, you know, I have the um, skills for this job."*
*Strong affirmative delivery: "I know that I have the skills for this job."*

*Watch the pitch of your voice. If your pitch is too high, you will sound like you are not confident or sure of yourself.*

*Try to do the interview in person, not over the telephone.*

*Do not be afraid to ask the interviewer to repeat a question if you do not understand it.*

*Do not use too many "feeling" words.*

*Weak delivery: "I feel that I would be good for this job" or "I think I have the qualifications."*
*Strong affirmative delivery: "I would be good for this job." "I have the qualifications."*

*Try to avoid clearing your throat as this will make you sound hesitant. Instead swallow or take a deep breath.*

## 10.13

# DRUG TESTING

Drug testing is the last thing you think about when you interview for a job but it is the first test you will take upon receiving an offer. The job market is heating up after a four-year recession. Companies are definitely hiring, and for some candidates, job offers are coming in much sooner than they expected. That's a good thing, but there can be some speed bumps along the way.

Rare is the job seeker who has not been exposed to recreational or bodybuilding drug use. The FBI had to alter their drug screening policy to be able to hire young agents. To be considered for employment recruits must have no marijuana use for the past 3 years and no other illegal drug use including steroids within the past 10 years. Even the last three US presidents have admitted occasional drug use in their youth.

In the midst of your college days, it is hard to think about the consequences of your recreational activities. After all, most people in college are young, on their own, and responsible for no one but themselves. But at a certain point, everyone has to grow up and stop engaging in high-risk behaviors.

Employment pre-screening includes drug tests, as well as credit, DMV, and criminal record checks. Breaking a leg snowboarding; getting arrested for drunk driving or texting while driving; or being rejected from a job after testing positive on a drug test are sobering and maturing experiences.

Just because everyone else does it does not

mean you should or that you will get away with it. Things have a way of catching up with scuff-laws. Although you are not running for president, you are applying for jobs with companies who want to hire responsible people to represent them in a positive light.

A positive drug test is a deal breaker. No one will hire you after you test positive. The risks are just too high. After you are employed, you can be fired for drug use. No company wants to incur the costs of having a drug user on board and many test their employees randomly. Same thing with drunk driving and texting while driving.

It is not just about your performance at work-- it is also the risk you pose to projects and the job site. And they also have to worry about the cost of your health care if you are going to endanger yourself.

Even if you are not using drugs, you can get caught in the net. Companies are testing for drug use and they are using increasingly sensitive tests to detect, not only your drug use, but also your exposure to drugs at parties.

I counseled a candidate to reject a fabulous offer from one of the most sought after multinational corporations: Bechtel. He was given an offer and told to go within a day to a local medical lab to submit for a drug test. It happened so fast that his head was spinning.

He knew he would not pass the test, but he really wanted the job. I suggested that he didn't need the stigma attached to a positive drug test.

Here is how it will happen. You think it will be weeks before you are hired. You meet with a company at a job fair, there is a positive connection and you go for an interview. You interview well, and you are given an offer on the spot or in a day or two. All of a sudden, you are in a dilemma. As soon as you accept the offer, you will be required to go for a drug test. You were at a party and you smoked marijuana last weekend, and Bam! It strikes you. You will not be able to pass the drug test.

It is hard to say with certainty how long drugs will remain in your system. A lot of things factor into the positive drug test equation – the type of drug used, the amount used, frequency of use, body fat and metabolism of the user. It also depends on what type of test is administered: urine, saliva, hair, blood, or sweat patch. Residuals from some drugs show up in sophisticated tests months after use.

You should expect to have your urine, your blood and your hair tested. Even if you are not using marijuana yourself, your hair can retain the drug if you are present where it was being smoked.

What should you do right now? Grow up! Stop taking drugs! Stop hanging around people who do! If you drink, do so in moderation, and under no circumstances should you drive, even if you have had only a little alcohol. Stop texting while driving! These things are all within your ability.

There is no reason to mess around unless you like the idea of being long-term unemployed. Companies will cut you no slack on stupid behavior that can cause accidents on the road or liability in the office. For an employer assessing whether or not to hire you past behavior is a strong predictor of future activity. Get caught once and you are in for a whole lot of heartbreak for a long time to come.

If you do have an immediate situation that is going to give you heartache, find a career counselor immediately who will help you troubleshoot the best course of action. There are things you can do before you accept the job offer. Once you have accepted the offer, things move way too fast to salvage the situation.

# SALARY NEGOTIATIONS

## 11.0

# SALARY NEGOTIATIONS: GETTING PAID WHAT YOU ARE WORTH

*Getting paid what you are worth is essential to your career health! Negotiating is a skill and an art, and you are going to learn how to negotiate for the salary you deserve.*

*Salary discussions are one of the final steps in the job search process.* Until the employer has actually made you an offer, you are not going to ask what a job pays and you are not going to discuss what you want. If the offer is lower than you expected, you need to be prepared to make the next move. It starts with the question: "Is That Salary Negotiable?"

But before you ask that question, you need to do your homework. When it comes to getting paid what you are really worth, you can't just guess. You won't be prepared unless you: first research current salary data, second itemize your assets relative to the particular position, and third compute your worth.

Computing your worth is going to involve some additional calculations. Every job offer brings with it positives and negatives that have to be figured into your ultimate negotiating position and final decision.

After you have determined that a potential employer is open to negotiations, and after you have done your homework, you have to have a negotiating strategy.

We are going to walk through the entire process, step-by-step. And just in case you are feeling intimidated by asking for more or for what you are worth, I'm going to say a few words about why it is so important that you get paid what you should be paid and how society and individuals suffer when employees don't receive fair salaries.

## 11.1

# IS THAT SALARY NEGOTIABLE?

One of the most frequent requests that I receive from individuals seeking my advice is how to negotiate their salary. The question often comes up during a job search, and later, when individuals want to renegotiate their salary. What you are paid is largely determined by the quality of the information you have regarding your worth to a company, and by your willingness to ask for what you are worth. Being able to demonstrate and document your value is exceedingly important.

In salary negotiations, *Rule Number One: never try to negotiate a salary until you have received an offer of employment.* Job applicants are often asked to provide a salary expectation or a salary history. I always advise job seekers not to respond to a verbal inquiry or on an application form. Instead, I recommend that you simply say that your salary demands are negotiable. When pressed I suggest that you indicate that salary is not your primary concern at this point and explain that you are focusing on the learning experience you will have and the challenges you will face. Indicate that you expect that you and they will reach a reasonable salary agreement after you have had a full understanding of the opportunity the company offers and after they have a complete sense of the skills and experience you bring to the table.

Why wait? Why not just blurt out what you

want at the offset? If you quote a salary that is too high, you will bid yourself out of the market. If you quote a salary that is too low, the prospective employer will believe that you do not understand the nature of the position, or that you are not really worth much, or that you are too anxious or too inexperienced for them to bother with. Why should they place a premium value on your expertise if you don't? You are in a much more powerful position when you have an offer in hand - after the employer knows exactly what you bring to the table, and after you know exactly what interesting challenges the job opportunity offers and what it entails.

The personnel folks may push for an answer about what you expect in your first interview, so you will probably need to be creative in fending them off. How should you approach the situation so as to not put the employer off? Tell them that you are flexible and that you really prefer to negotiate your salary after you have a complete understanding of the position. Say something like "At this point I am really more concerned about the learning experience I will have and the type of work I will do. I think we can come to a reasonable agreement about salary after I understand all that this position offers and you have a sense of the talent that I bring with me."

*Rule Number Two: do your homework!* There are three basic pieces of information that you need to develop before you respond to any questions about salary expectations.

FIRST, you need information on competitive salaries for people already in the labor market who have skills, experience, and training similar to yours. (Salaries differ greatly from city to city, state to state, and country to country. This has to do with the cost of living and the supply and demand for different professionals and specific skills sets).

SECOND, you need to develop a list of your assets and abilities. This helps you and the employer understand why you are worth what you are asking for. (You should chronicle your accomplishments on paper throughout your career so you will know and be able to share pertinent data when it is time to renegotiate and on what basis.)

THIRD, you need to do a cost of living survey for the cities where you might be living. I frequently work with candidates who have no idea about the worth of their salary offers in different cities nor the cost of living in various cities. This is really important. Way too often individuals find that they have accepted an offer to move to a higher salaried position only to find that they will be living in a much higher cost living area. They are shocked to discover that they cannot afford the move.

*Rule Number Three: have a negotiating strategy.* Your decision to negotiate for a higher salary should only be made after you have received an offer and after you have done your research. If you feel your offer is not high enough now is the time to negotiate. Do not accept the job first and then try to get more money. Negotiate *before* you accept the offer. Timing and information are everything.

From your research, you should know what you are worth, what the market will bear, and the relative strength of your bargaining position.

When an unacceptable offer is made, your response is to ask: "Is that salary negotiable?" Your question is actually a statement ("I want more money"), but don't worry about this minor bit of miscommunication; the people on the other side of the table (or phone) will understand the question as a polite and proper opening move. Unless they tell you that the offer is the best they can do, they are undoubtedly going to counter with: "What did you have in mind?" When you hear that, the negotiations have been opened. You will be expected not only to give a figure of worth that you have arrived at, but you will also have to back it up with facts.

You will have to tell them what you want and why you deserve it. In essence, you have to explain the basis for your request and justify your demand.

This is where your research pays off. In addition to the information you have gathered about what you are worth to them you will be expected to identify the elements that make you an exceptional candidate.

During your job search you should be applying for multiple positions so that you have some options and hopefully receive multiple offers. This puts you in a much more powerful negotiating position. The easiest way to make your case for more money is by comparing their offer to other higher offers you have received.

When you present your opening salary request, it is usually best to go a little bit high so that you will have room for compromise. Go high, but be sure to keep it reasonable. And remember that you are not just talking about money. You have to evaluate the whole package, including benefits, opportunities, future potential, training, location, and so on. Be sure to have a folder with the salary information and a list of your assets to share with your employer.

Compromise is the key to good negotiations. You are looking for a challenging career with a competitive compensation package. Their interests are the same as yours: they want to pay you what you are worth so that they gain a committed employee. They want someone who is satisfied and who won't waste time and attention thinking about finding a better opportunity or leave when the market improves after they have trained you. To reach this common goal, there has to be flexibility on both sides of the table. Most companies are fairly motivated to negotiate especially if you are in a high demand field. This holds true for experienced as well as inexperienced candidates. The supply of talent worldwide is shrinking.

## 11.2

# SOURCES FOR RESEARCHING WHAT YOU ARE WORTH

## OCCUPATIONAL OUTLOOK HANDBOOK

Your market research begins by obtaining a benchmark on what recent college graduates are receiving. There are some fabulous sources for information on competitive salaries for every field imaginable. The web has a ton of sites with great salary information. *The Occupational Outlook Handbook is available online in it's entirety ... use the search box on the left.* This resource will give you vital information (including salary data) on numerous occupations including:

Nature of the Work
Training, Other Qualifications,
and Advancement
Employment
Job Outlook
Projections Data
Earnings
OES Data
Related Occupations
Sources of Additional Information

## SALARY.COM

Salary.com provides excellent salary and career planning information for the both inexperienced and experienced professionals. Be sure to use the free Salary Wizard. It allows you to collect salary data based not only on job title but also by zip code.

The information is organized by discipline and by location. Drill down and be creative in collecting information from this source. Search multiple job titles and be sure to read the job descriptions to be sure that the job title you are using as a benchmark corresponds to the job description for the job you are being considered for.

You will find that there is a fairly wide range of salaries for any given job title. For example when I searched for salaries for city planners in Oakland, CA, salaries ranged from $42,453 to $60,286. Why such a broad range for the same job? Because candidates range pretty broadly in their qualifications and because the potential employers range broadly in their ability to pay. We will get to that when we discuss your assets. It is definitely part of the equation.

Another thing, government typically pays less than private firms, but not always... And if you have a MS degree you will typically start higher on the pay scale and require less experience.

Here is the salary data and job info that I found at salary.com searching "city planner" in Oakland, CA:

Salary
*10th percentile: $42,453*
*25th percentile: $44,884*
*75th percentile: $54,209*
*90th percentile: $60,268*

*Job Description: Urban Planner*
Develops land-use plans for the beneficial development of urban areas. Requires a bachelor's degree in a related field and 2-4 years of experience in the field or in a related area. Familiar with standard concepts, practices, and procedures within a particular field. Relies on judgment and limited experience to plan and accomplish goals. Performs a variety of tasks. Works under general supervision; typically reports to a supervisor or manager. A certain degree of creativity and latitude is required.

A young business graduate named Stephanie received an offer of employment from a financial planning company that she believed was low at $40,000. She asked the manager making the offer if it was negotiable. All of the interviews had gone well, they liked her, and they were very motivated to hire her. The manager was intrigued and impressed with her request. He asked her what she felt she was worth and why she felt she was worth it. She said she was looking for $46,000 and gave her justification. She showed him the salary data she had collected during her research and she showed him a list of her assets highlighting her academic and employment achievements as well as her skills that matched the position's requirements. He bumped her salary to $46,000. She made $6000 in just moments by being well prepared and by asking!

## PROFESSIONAL ASSOCIATIONS & ORGANIZATIONS

Professional organizations associated with your field are another excellent source of both salary info and career information. For example the National Society for Professional Engineers survey their members and report salary information by education, experience, location, branch of engineering, industry and job function. I found the NSPE salary info at http://www.nspe.org. This organization requires that you pay for the survey. The Occupational Outlook Handbook will give you names of professional organizations in your field under "additional sources of information" under each job category.

## COMPANY & GOVERNMENT AGENCY WEB SITES

Company web sites can provide you with information on available positions. Few give salary ranges with jobs that they post. They will post complete job descriptions with job requirements.

State agencies are an excellent source for salary data. State and local government agencies are frequently mandated by law to pay employees wages that are competitive with the private sector. In California this is generally true.

## 11.3

# WHAT YOU BRING TO THE TABLE DETERMINES WHAT AN EMPLOYER WILL PAY YOU

## ITEMIZING YOUR ASSETS

It is time to get in touch with what makes you valuable to an employer. Making a list of your assets will help you lock in on just what makes you special for the position you are applying for.

*To begin with, review the job description carefully.* Dissect it and analyze the information. Highlight the "must haves" and the "preferred

qualifications". What critical knowledge and skills are they asking for? What makes you a strong candidate?

*Now select your top seven to ten strengths and list them bullet by bullet on a single piece of paper titled: Assets of Your Name- in big (24 point) bold letters.* You will be sharing these items with your potential employer when you are engaged in your salary negotiating meeting. These are the items that give the employer the essential information they need to pay you the big bucks. What is special about you relative to the position you are pursuing?

Be sure to quantify where possible and to put the information in descending order of importance according to the employer's priorities.

**Examples:**

*Assets of Elizabeth Matti*
- MS in Urban Planning - UCLA (GPA 3.95)
- BS Political Science - UC Berkeley (GPA 3.98)
- 2 years of internship experience with state and local government agencies
- Exceptional writing skills
- Well-refined research and analysis skills
- Experience in developing positive community relations
- Specialized coursework in city and regional planning; urban sociology; cities, space and society

*Assets of Raymond Ward*
- BS EE, GPA 3.9
- 9.5 years experience in operations
- Graduated #1 from USAF Leadership School
- 5 years - first line supervisor
- 2 years - managing work center
- Exceptional leadership, communication
- Well-refined organization and time management skills

# 11.4

# COMPUTING YOUR WORTH

Your relative value is determined by a combination of the assets you bring with you as you can see in examples in 11.3.

*Your assets include:*
- your education (including degrees and specialized coursework)
- your specialized expertise
- your experience
- your skills (such as communication, organization, analysis etc.)
- military experience
- maturity
- foreign language skills

***Things external to you also enter the salary equation.*** The company size, the company's particular industry niche, the general economy (supply/demand), and the geographic location of your potential employer all play a role in the salary you will receive. The impact of these factors is constantly changing, and therefore, you need to stay current with your information. As an example, it used to be that salaries in Sacramento were discounted relative to the San Francisco Bay Area. Today in Sacramento salaries are quite close to those in the Bay Area.

***Every company negotiates if they want you bad enough.*** A computer science graduate that I worked with a number of years ago received offers of $60K in the San Francisco Bay Area and an offer of $54K in Folsom at Intel Corporation. Intel initially told him the offer was not negotiable, but when he started his negotiations he shared the info on the other offers he had received and Intel immediately matched them. This holds true even more so today with an increasing demand and diminishing supply of talent. The more offers you have the better. In other words, you can use higher salary offers to leverage offers where the job description or location might be more attractive but the offer is lower. Although the San Francisco area is a higher cost of living area employers in surrounding areas compete for talent and must offer salaries that are competitive to attract the talent they need.

You can be a lot more flexible with your salary demands if you live in an area with a lower cost of living. In such an area, you can't necessarily expect as much, but you won't actually need as much. A good source for cost of living information is the "Places Rated Almanac" by Savageau and Boyer. You can find the book at Amazon.com. This publication ranks about 350 metropolitan areas, comparing living costs, employment outlook, housing, transportation, education, health care, crime, recreation and climate.

I typed "salaries in different cities" into a Google search and the first site that came up was a great source: CNN Money. This site allows you to input a salary offer in one city and see what salary you would need to meet the buying power of that salary in another city. Maybe you know how far your salary goes in one place and you need to know what kind of offer you would need to have a similar lifestyle in the other city.

One job seeker I worked with had had little luck finding work by the time I met him six months after graduation. After we revised his resume and his job search strategy he immediately had interviews with four companies and two offers within a couple of weeks. He had one offer in Texas and one offer in California. The Texas offer was $20,000 less that the salaries for the same type of position in California.

Companies are looking for a combination of skills and abilities that make their companies successful. Couple that with the fact that huge numbers of baby boomers are retiring and the bottom line is they need you!

If you have the right stuff they want you and they are willing to pay for your talents. Amazingly- you are more often than not, in the driver's seat.

I worked with an experienced candidate in Houston who was offered a job with Siemens, a large, multinational firm. The job offer included a better work schedule, it was closer to home, and at a significantly higher salary. The offer came through a former co-worker who had joined Siemens earlier in the year. When he submitted his resignation to his current employer they begged him for the chance to renegotiate the terms of his employment to keep him on board. He was stunned. The new offer motivated his current employer to work hard to keep him. The company exceeded all aspects of the international firm's offer. They arranged for him to work from home multiple days per week and increased his salary by 45% above the salary he had been working at in the same position. The fear of losing a really great employee motivated his employer to sweeten the pot to keep him. He liked the company and his co-workers and really didn't want to leave his employer so he agreed to stay.

*If the company you are negotiating with does not meet your expectations on the salary side, and they are unwilling to negotiate, you can explore other aspects of the package. Perhaps they can offer other inducements.* Some companies pay tuition for your graduate degree. Other companies pay off student loans. I have also heard of companies offering additional weeks of vacation to entice a candidate. Signing bonuses, retention bonuses, and moving expenses are also common. There are also many things that you may consider advantageous like on site child care or adult care for family members that might make the salary less important.

Maybe they can give you an office, instead of a cubicle, or perhaps there is a stock option sweetener. Yes, even if the stock market is down at the moment in time when you are negotiating, it will go up eventually. Keep in mind that all of those Ferraris down in Silicon Valley were paid for with stock that was owned before the company went public.

*The final task is knowing when to say "yes" and when to walk away.* Actually, this is something that you should have known from the beginning. Before you even ask if it's negotiable, you need to know your bottom line. It may change while you talk - as more information is thrown into the discussion - but you need to have dollar amount in mind

*You can do this. Just remember, be reasonable, be informed, don't be greedy, and most importantly, don't be afraid to ask.*

## 11.5

# WHY IS WHAT YOU ARE PAID SO IMPORTANT?

Getting paid what you are worth is extremely important to your career success. Your first job and the salary you are paid after finishing college frequently sets the tone for your entire career. Think about it, every time your salary is computed for a raise and every time you are considered for a promotion your job titles and salary history are used to come up with a decision on whether you should be hired, promoted, or receive a raise as well as how much that raise should be.

What you are paid determines both how you will live and your potential career growth over time. In this culture your career is a huge part of your identity. Getting a competitive salary is an equity issue. Set your standard. Figure out what you are worth. If you undervalue yourself other people will undervalue you. You are the person who is in control of your value.

If you have done your homework you should be in a position to decide whether an offer is acceptable based on solid information gained from your research.

Accepting a bad offer can slow your career way down or even sour you on your field. Think about it. You have spent countless hours in college developing knowledge and skills preparing yourself for a career. You may also have some significant work experience. How long did it take to get your degree and qualifications? Do you really want to jump at a substandard job offer? Wouldn't it be a good idea to invest some time in your job search just as you have in your education? Rejecting offers that do not meet your minimum standards allows you the time you need to continue looking for the job that is right for you.

When the market is tight you hear repeatedly that jobs are scarce and that you should grab what you can get. But even in the tightest market there are jobs for qualified candidates who know how to look, and where to look for good jobs. There is always a market for talented individuals. If you do not know how to look, hire a career coach.

Do you have to start at the bottom? Absolutely not. As a matter of fact, if you start your career at the bottom of an organization you will most likely stay there. You will get pegged as a low achiever. Yes, there are stories about people who have managed to climb in an organization from administrative assistant or janitor to CEO but they are few and far between, and I have yet to meet any of them.

It can take nerves of steel to reject an unacceptable position or to negotiate for the best possible salary. It also takes confidence that

something better will come along if you reject a substandard offer. Sometimes it is the job of the career coach to give people permission to reject unacceptable offers. You can give yourself permission if you know the job is not right. Why settle for something you know will fail? Keep looking until you find the right job. The payoff: you get a job where you can thrive.

It is a well worn myth that you should "just get in" and then move up. Great companies need talent to keep their businesses running. Companies hire college graduates from a variety of majors into all kinds of great professional trainee positions.

I worked with an extremely talented young woman who was selling herself short by applying for jobs well below her level of competence. She had just returned to the US from Australia where she had played on a national water polo team after graduating from college. Upon returning to the US, after two years of international competition, she was ready to put her degree in business management to work. She wanted a job in high-end fashion retail management but figured she would have to start at the bottom as a sales clerk anywhere she could get in.

I explained to her that companies do not post all of their positions on their web sites. I suggested that rather than starting as a retail sales clerk, that she could target her most desirable company first and start her career as a retail "management trainee".

She was hired within days of our work together into a dream job in the exclusive high fashion department at Nordstrom's in San Francisco. We worked for a total of four hours developing a career focus, a targeted resume and a solid career plan. It took no time at all. She didn't have settle for "just getting in".

She parlayed that job into a position with one of the most recognizable international fashion houses in the world - Alexander McQueen.

One of the saddest stories I have to tell is about another young woman who undervalued herself when applying for jobs and negotiating her starting salary. She called me four years after she had languished in a position way beneath her level to ask for career advice regarding her position with a high tech firm. As a new electronics engineering graduate, she was hired at the same time as male classmates. When asked by the interviewer what her salary expectations were she quoted a salary of half of the competitive salaries for electronics engineers. She was insecure about her knowledge and skills, even though she had graduated with honors and had had several internships in the field. Her reasoning was that the employer expectations would be lower if she asked for less and so she would be under less pressure. After she got hired she figured that she would be able to prove her worth and recover to reach salary parody later.

Four years later when she called and indicated that she was still severely underpaid and that she was never given anything but technician level work to do. She was underpaid and undervalued. Now she was asking me what she should do. She was underemployed and her knowledge was stale. She had not gotten the opportunity to develop or update her skills over time with challenging work or training available to the engineers. I helped her untangle herself from the mess she had gotten into.

*The serious job seeker sets their goals at an appropriately high level, commensurate with their education, skills and experience.* I often hear people say, "I will take an administrative position and work my way up" or "I will take a technician level position just to get my foot in the door". That may work occasionally for some people but it is a very circuitous path to getting where you want to be. Aim for the dust and you will end up in the dust. My advice is to set your goals and aim for where you want to be if you

ever hope to get there.

Sometimes looking for work requires surviving while you are looking. You may wish to take a survival job that allows you to pay your bills but also affords you the time to look for an appropriate career position.

## 11.6

# SURVIVAL JOB

***What is a survival job?*** It is a part time position in food service that supports your job search. A survival job is a job that pays you a sustenance wage- just enough to get by and make do. You should not become comfortable with a survival job. Discomfort is one of the great motivators — you need to be highly motivated to do the things required to find an appropriate career position. It is also a job that does not consume all of the available time. It might be an off hour job- nights or weekends, leaving enough of the regular, standard daytime working hours to look for work. Because your primary objective is to get a great job, you do not want your survival job to overpower or undermine your search. A survival job just finances your search. It should not impede your search.

There are other ways to support your job search. Some people use savings. Other people have family, parents or spouses, that help support them during the job search. As I have said before, the average length of time you need to find a career position is three to six months if you are a serious job seeker - looking full time and using the right techniques.

11.7

# INDIVIDUALS AND SOCIETY SUFFER WHEN PEOPLE ARE UNDERPAID

*Inadequate pay impacts both men and women, and it hurts American families.* Since the 1970's, it has required two wage earners to support a reasonable middle class family life style. With inflation and economic conditions worsening, very few families can afford to have only one person bringing home a paycheck. It is your job to make sure that you are getting an equitable wage for the work you do. If you do not do your homework you and your family stand to lose.

Both men and women need to be armed with information about their worth and their assets to ensure that they receive an appropriate salary.

Unfortunately there is a huge discrepancy in what people in the same positions are paid in many work environments. Failing to get the info you need to negotiate effectively is lethal. This is particularly true for women. Women are paid about 77% of what men are paid for working full time, according to a 2005 US Bureau of Labor Statistics report. Minority women are paid even less. It all starts quite early in the career cycle. According to National Association of Colleges and Employers, at the entry level, male college graduates typically receive more than female college graduates. And we know that just with compound interest, the differences are amplified over the years.

It is true in the private and public sectors: women do not receive equal pay for equal work. The cumulative effect is devastating and it is long lasting. In the short term pay disparity affects a candidate's spending power and in the long term it diminishes their retirement earnings. It is a huge looming crisis for baby-boomers who are beginning to wonder how they will be able to save enough money and accrue enough earnings to see them through their retirement years.

According to the National Organization for Women, "If women received the same wages as men who work the same number of hours, have the same education and union status, are the same age, and live in the same region of the country, then these women's annual income would rise by $4,000 and poverty rates would be cut in half. Working families would gain an astounding $200 billion in family income annually."

Consider the case of Lilly Ledbetter, a supervisor for GM who was paid 15% to 25% less than her male counterparts, including those with significantly less experience than her. Although GM has a strict policy of secrecy on salaries, with employees forbidden to discuss their salaries, Lilly Ledbetter received an anonymous letter indicating that she had been underpaid for 19 years at GM. She filed a lawsuit and a jury awarded her a $3 million settlement. A judge cut that ruling from $3 million to $360,000 due to the limitation inserted into the Civil Rights Act of 1991 during the first Bush administration.

GM pursued the issue all the way to the US Supreme Court. The Court ruled that even though she was not aware of the discrepancy for 19 years, she had to file her suit within 180 days of when it occurred for the very first time. The 2007 ruling effectively says that if you can keep it a secret, you can get away with paying less to women and minorities.

Typically, wage disparity is considered to be an issue in the private sector, a problem that does not exist in public employment. That, however, is not the case. In public employment situations, it can happen in much more subtle ways. In public employment, wage disparity discrimination is accomplished under the table through classification and promotion practices.

Secrecy is not a good thing, as was discovered by Lilly Ledbetter. Secrecy gives license for unequal treatment. What we need is transparency. One engineer I know who works in private industry has long made it his practice to tell his colleagues what he earns. His view is that he does not wish to be part of a conspiracy of secrecy, and he wants his fellow workers to have the opportunity to negotiate on equal footing. He is committed to sunshine and transparency in the workplace.

## 11.8

# "WHAT ARE YOUR SALARY REQUIREMENTS?" A QUESTION YOU SHOULD NEVER ANSWER!

Job seekers frequently find themselves in a tight situation when it comes to the salary question. Your resume is out there and sometimes calls come out of the blue. You are invited to apply for a specific position because someone has recommended you. The invitation may include a request that you tell them how much you expect to be paid. It might be a verbal request for information, or a question on the application, or it might be an email request for your salary expectations.

Failure to do this right means you do not know how the game is played. Let me explain.

Salary is only one aspect of a job. There are many other factors that will impact your satisfaction with a particular position. You need to have complete information on all that is offered by the job and the organization before you make your salary demands known. You need to be presented with the entire package - salary, benefits, location, growth opportunities, the people you will work with, the perks and so much more... You are looking at a career, not a job. It may bring with it a whole new life in a whole new place. You need to see the whole picture to really know what you are looking at. And they need to understand all that you bring to the table.

Do not tell a potential employer what salary you expect before you have been made an offer! (You do not really know yet). Do not tell them what you want! And never, never, never give your salary history. Your previous salary might be completely unrelated to the position you are seeking - like that food service position that paid for your education. If your experience is related you may have been an underpaid intern. Or the job you previously held might have been in a low cost of living area and the new job is in a high cost of living area. You might scare them away if they think you were overpaid. Why give them info that will ratchet down your salary or scare them off? Tell them you are n-e-g-o-t-i-a-b-l-e... (Learn how to spell it!) and at this point you need more information to make a good decision.

Although this might seem like an adversarial situation, or that I am advising you to be argumentative, this is actually a mutually beneficial approach. You need more information. They need to get the best possible candidate. That can only happen when everyone has all the details and data.

Ask the Headhunter Nick Corcodilos put it quite clearly: "employers who insist are a bad risk ... why work for someone who tries to force you to share private information that has no bearing on your interview, on your value, on whether you get an offer, or on what the new salary offer is? ... when you disclose your salary information, your negotiating leverage is gone. Your salary history is not any employer's business. Always decline to disclose, politely but firmly. No matter what they say, no matter what they threaten."

Employers ask this question simply because they are in the habit of asking this question. Somewhere along the line, it became common knowledge among recruiters that this is a question that should be asked.

It is a useful question when recruiters and headhunters are seeking to lure high-value employees away from one company and place them in another. It is a useful question when a headhunter is asking: "what will it take to get you to move?" But when you are responding to an ordinary job opportunity, there is no good reason for the question to be asked and a number of good reasons why you should not answer.

In reality, it is never a useful question.

If a recruiter comes to you asking you to become the new CEO of General Motors, you are not going to tell them anything about your salary requirements. If you are qualified for that position, you are going to wait and see what they offer, and then you are going to negotiate.

The same thing is true for any other job. Your job is to tell them what you have to offer, what you bring to the table, and why they should hire you.

If they put a price on the job offer in advance - they advertised the salary they were willing to pay and you applied, indicating that you were willing to accept that salary - then the negotiations are done, more or less (actually, you are still going to ask if that salary is negotiable before you accept the offer).

But if they left it open, asking what you want,

then they have asked you to set the starting price. And they have asked you to set the starting price before you know how much they value your credentials or what you are worth to them. They are asking you to put a price on your talent based on how desperate you are to obtain work, rather than on what you are actually worth to them.

There are in fact a number of ways you can obtain information about what your experience and credentials are worth. There are great salary estimators available on the web (see 11.2 about career/salary research).

But when you are applying for a job or responding to an inquiry, it is not the time to tell anyone what you are willing to accept or how much money you require.

There is a time to negotiate salary. It is not when you are submitting your application. You negotiate your salary when the employer is ready to make a commitment to you and when you are willing to make a commitment to them. You don't discuss your salary requirements until they have expressed an interest in closing the deal.

Never tell a prospective employer anything about your salary requirements. You do not really know enough about the position until you have gone through the entire process and interview process. Be patient. You need to know what the critical skills are that they are looking for, how you meet their needs, and what the total package looks like. It is not just about salary, it is also about benefits, living costs and future potential. When you have all of the information, that is when you will know how to value yourself and how to value the opportunity. Then you can negotiate.

When they ask you how much you want? You tell them: "Right now I am interested in finding out about the position and gaining a full understanding of the responsibilities as well as in sharing my background and qualifications. I think when we both have a fuller understanding of what the position entails and what I bring to the table, we will be able to reach a reasonable agreement."

Making a premature bid is just a really bad idea. Bid too low, it tells them you are not worth much, or that you do not know what you are worth. Either way you are demonstrating that you are not the brightest bulb or the fastest chip. Bid too high, they will know that you are not in contact with reality.

Let the employer make the opening bid, after they know who you are. The employer is the one who has the information necessary to determine what it is worth to them to hire you. You will have plenty of opportunity to let them know what the job is worth to you.

# 12

# REFERENCES

**12.0**

# WHAT IS A GOOD REFERENCE & WHAT SHOULD YOU GIVE YOUR REFERENCES?

Your references are one of your most important assets in the job search. The comments of a good reference can spur an employer into selecting you over other candidates. The comments of a bad reference can nix the offer in an instant.

If you are planning to interview for professional career positions in the near future it is time to get your references lined up! You will need three to five professional references. They need to be good references who will sing your praises.

To begin with, you will want to create a document that uses the header from your resume. Just below your resume header (that includes your name, address, phone, and email), the reference page will be titled "References" and will have two columns. One column will have the name, title, organization, address, phone, and email address of each of your references and it will appear as you would address an envelope. The second column will have a description of how you know the person. For example: Supervisor on bridge project; Sr. Project Professor; Co-team member on Sr. Design project; Co-worker at Air Resources, Inc.

A good professional reference is a person you ask, and who agrees, to allow you to use their name as a person who can be called upon to speak about your good professional qualities. Contact anyone you plan to use and ask if they would be willing to let you use them as a reference. Don't use anyone who you don't ask first and make sure that they will say only good things about you.

*People who qualify to give you a good reference:*

• A professor who you have gotten a good grade from
• A former or current employer or supervisor who knows the quality of your work
• A co-worker who likes working with you
• A sr. project co-team member (who doesn't hate you yet...)

*Do not use:*
• Family members
• Friends
• People who don't know you professionally

*Give all of your references a file folder with your name on the tab containing:*

• A recent picture of yourself
• A resume
• A list of your strengths
• A list of your interests
• A list of the types of positions for which you are applying
• A list of the companies that may be contacting them

References need to have all of these things in order to give you a good reference. Some calls for references come months or years later when you are all but forgotten.

Employers will ask you for references and they will call! Keep in touch with your references and keep them posted on your progress. You will be glad you did!

# GIVE TO YOUR REFERENCE

Hi Cici,

This is Sam Chao from Alpha Team. As you requested I have compiled information that will help you give me a good reference. I have also attached my resume.

My technical skills:
*Problem Solving*
*Coding*
*GUI Design*
*System Software*
*Management Skill*
*Database Applications*
*Software Detail Design*
*There are more in my resume as well.*

My interests:
*Software Applications*
*System Software*
*Database Design*
*Networking*
*Software Development*

My responsibilities in JFESS project are:
*Designed Graphical User Interface (GUI) for the system.*
*Coded two modules:*
*Taking data from the database - put it into the Excel file for survey's reports.*
*Taking data from the database - put it into the Excel file for webmaster posting the information on the web.*

Beside that I was responsible for:
*Managed group meetings and handled project risk management.*
*Initially designed and created the JFESS database.*
*Partially involved in most aspects of the software lifecycle.*
*Recommend the best solutions for the team.*

Those are my strengths and my responsibilities in the JFESS project.
Thank you very much.

Sincerely,
Sam Chao

## 12.2    SAMPLE REFERENCE PAGE

Christine Young
869 Sesame Street, Sacramento CA 95821

| REFERENCES | RELATIONSHIP |
|---|---|
| Bridget Smith, Associate Engineer<br>City of Sacramento<br>Public Works Department, Traffic Services<br>1000 I Street, Suite 170<br>Sacramento, CA 95819<br>(916) 264-7508<br>brdgetS@email.com | Supervisor &  co-worker<br>in Traffic Engineering<br>Department |
| Marty Hanneman, City Traffic Engineer<br>City of Sacramento<br>Public Works Department, Traffic Services<br>1000 I Street, Suite 170<br>Sacramento, CA 95819<br>(916) 264-7508<br>MartyH@email.com | Office Manager |
| Greg Smith, Engineering Aide<br>City of Sacramento<br>Public Works Department, Traffic Services<br>1000 I Street, Suite 170<br>Sacramento, CA 95819<br>(916) 264-8364<br>GregS@email.com | Supervisor & co-worker<br>in Traffic Engineering<br>Department |
| Shakir Shatnawi, Ph.D.<br>California State University, Sacramento<br>6000 J Street<br>Sacramento, CA 95819<br>(916) 227-7306<br>ShakirS@email.com | Professor, CE 147,<br>Highway Design Class |

13

# WHICH OFFER SHOULD YOU TAKE?

13.0

# WHICH OFFER SHOULD YOU TAKE?

When you start your job search you will want to apply for positions in a variety of different places. That means that you will probably receive more than one offer of employment during your search. There is risk involved in accepting the wrong offer so assessing each opportunity carefully and deciding which offer to take is critical. Once you accept an offer, you are actually removing yourself from the market. You are saying, I am no longer seeking a job. I have found what I want.

There are things you can to do to assess the viability of accepting a particular offer.

No matter how up or down the market is, there are jobs out there and people are getting hired. There is always opportunity for good candidates. Even in the tightest market qualified candidates still get good offers and have to make decisions on which offer to take or what their timing should be in accepting an offer.

It would be nice if all of the offers came in at the same time. It would be nice if you could set each one on the table and carefully compare it with every other offer you've received. Better yet, wouldn't it be nice if you could plug all the data in and let your computer tell you what moves to make next in your life? But it seldom happens that way. Most of the time the offers straggle in and the less desirable ones arrive first.

Job seekers are always tempted to grab the first thing that comes along. But that is not always the best course of action. Sometimes it pays to slow the pace and assess the offer and to reject offers that do not meet with your requirements. Yes, you need to have minimum requirements as to which offer to accept just as employers have minimum requirements for which candidate to hire.

One candidate that I worked with was interviewed by a human resources outsourcing company. His antenna went up instantly as he was greeted by the interview team. The interviewers were dressed in shorts and flip flops. As the interview progressed he was not impressed. The team spoke about the youth culture, heavy partying and the need for someone to fit in. Everyone he saw was under 30. He was young, dressed in a suit and interested in a professional position. This looked like a really flaky company to him. During the interview he kept looking for a way out. Trusting his instincts, he emailed the interviewers when he arrived home and requested that his name be removed from consideration. He had been looking for a job for about six months so he was highly motivated to accept any reasonable offer. But as he assessed the situation, he realized that a position with this company would not take him where he wanted to go. He decided unemployment represented a better option than joining that zoo.

Sometimes you just know things are not right. It is better to keep looking for the right job. Trust your instincts. If it is not right, walk away. You can make the decision to do so. It is important for any candidate to trust their instincts. You know when a job is not a match made in heaven.

Once you accept an inferior offer, it is really difficult, if not impossible, to continue your search for the right job. Taking the wrong job is like putting on handcuffs, you feel trapped. You feel like you have no options. Once you start a job you incur obligations- rent, car payments, credit card debt for the wardrobe you need, and the stuff you want.

There are not enough hours in a day to learn a new job, perform well in a sub-standard environment and look for a better position. It is emotionally and physically exhausting. So by accepting a substandard job you are handicapping your chances of finding the right job.

Untangling yourself from a job you hate is dicey. You will not perform at your optimum while you are in a job you don't like or working with people you do not respect. Setting up interviews while you are being watched over as the "new kid on the block" will not be easy either. And you have to explain to the next employer why you are leaving your job so soon. Then there are the reference checks...

Getting the right job is like finding the right tennis partner. Your performance depends on playing with the best partners. You need to be challenged.

## 13.1

## ASSESSING THE OFFERS

More jobs are offered to job applicants and new college graduates during the spring than at any other time of the year. This is when employers fill new positions and cultivate new employees. Many candidates are in the enviable, but difficult position of selecting between competing offers and figuring out who they will allow to employ them.

As exciting as it is to get more than one offer it is a stressful time because there are so many opportunities and so many decisions to make. Where will you start your career or your next career job? Where will you start your life or move your life? Who will be part of your life? You are going to spend more of your waking time with the people you work with than the people you choose to marry or partner with. Think about it... You will definitely want to decide carefully who you want to work with.

I have coached many individuals through this process over the years, and as exciting as it is to be wanted by many companies, it is also nerve racking. You have to worry that you might make the wrong decision.

I worked with one individual who was deciding between multiple offers in multiple locations. He was concerned he might make the wrong decision. He wanted to know if I had ever seen a person who later regretted the decision that they had made.

In my experience, the biggest regret that people have in this situation is leaving a loved one behind, assuming they just need a job, forgetting that they are starting a life. I have received frantic calls from individuals who have said, "I left my girlfriend or boyfriend back in California, and now I miss them so much, I realize that I don't want a life without them."

Another regret is moving to the wrong location. People mistakenly think that they can live anywhere if they just have a job, forgetting that they also need a life. One individual called from Hobbs, New Mexico. He was making tons of money wildcatting for Schlumberger, a major supplier of technology to the oil and gas industry. He was driving around with a crew of guys drilling for oil in the desert. When he called, he said, "Get me out of Hobbs, New Mexico. There are no women here!"

Deciding which offer to take is a two-step process. The first step requires personal reflection and introspection as to what you want in life. This is your self- assessment. The second step requires a careful analysis of the options.

**13.2**

# SELF ASSESSMENT FOR OFFER DECISIONS

*List your goals and set your priorities.* The first thing you need to do when faced with a major decision in life is to list your goals. Putting things down on paper clarifies the issues.

You need it on paper to actually see what is really important to you. This list should include personal as well as professional goals. If you have an important other that you would like to share your life with, it is good to factor in their goals, or at least discuss the big decision together. If you want to stay in a relationship, you need to have common or compatible goals.

After listing your goals, set your priorities. Forget the less important goals and focus on the most important. A good method to identify your most important goals is to label them as A goals or B goals, and then number them (A1, A2, A3 etc.). Focus on the A goals. (This is explained in detail in Chapter 6.5).

List your workstyle and lifestyle priorities. What do you need to start your career? Your work style list should include things you need to thrive at work such as: a good training program, a good team of professionals to work with, a boss who empowers you (if you are pursuing a professional license like with engineers or psychologists you definitely need your boss to be a licensed professional in your field, under whom you will work and receive qualifying hours of supervision), good technical support and equipment, a clear corporate mission statement, a competitive salary with great benefits, and a chance to apply what you have learned in your education. Prioritize the list.

Your lifestyle list should include things you need to thrive outside of work. What should you include? Well, your list might include: affordable housing, a reasonable commute, a livable community, quality schools, a low crime rate, a major university where you can continue your education, proximity to family, being close to your "important other", a short drive to the ski slopes and an even shorter drive to the ocean. Include whatever you need to feel like life is good and not just all work. I worked with an electrical engineer, who loved surfing and number one on his priority list was that he be able to surf from time to time. He now works as a design engineer at Port Hueneme, California, and he surfs during lunchtime everyday. This is one happy camper!

Once you have done your personal reflection by listing your goals and your lifestyle/work style preferences, set your priorities. Now you have criteria by which to assess which offer represents the best possible move for your career and your life.

**13.3**

# QUANTITATIVE ANALYSIS FOR JOB OFFERS

When you have received an offer, you will need to decide if it is a good offer for you. A quantitative analysis is the best way to approach the decision. Many people I have worked with are delighted to hear that this task can be broken down into numbers.

Take a piece of paper and divide it into two columns, labeling one column "pros," and one column "cons." Then, make a list of the pros and the cons of the offer. These will include things that relate to your goals and work/lifestyle preferences. Then, adjacent to each item, assign a numerical value on a scale from one to ten: how important is that item? Do this analysis for each offer you receive and you will now have a way to choose between the offers.

One IT professional that I worked with a couple of years ago had an offer from a company in San Francisco that was several thousand dollars higher than another offer she had from the Franchise Tax Board (FTB) in Sacramento.

She was very nervous about taking an offer that was lower. After she finished doing the analysis, she was able to see that the FTB offer represented the best professional and personal move for her and her family.

A construction management candidate had multiple offers to compare. *(see sample of job comparison p.174 )*

Another individual was deciding between a military career and a civilian job offer with a defense contractor. *(see sample of job comparison p.174 )*

## SAMPLE OF QUANTITATIVE ANALYSIS OF JOB OFFER COMPARISON ANALYZING OFFERS (P.174) ▶

**METHOD #1** *(Comparison Offers)*
**METHOD #2** *(Pros & Cons List)*

That is how you sort the offers and plan your career and your life!

## 13.4

# MAKING THE DECISION

Here is how it will happen. You interview well and come out with an offer. Now, faced with a decision, what do you do? You have an offer in hand and you have to decide if you really want it? Should you take it? Should you keep looking and try to find the perfect job? Do you really have the option to stall a company that has made you an offer especially in a tight or uncertain market?

Making such a big life decision is not easy. Every time you make a decision and choose one course of action, you give up every other choice. That which you give up represents your "opportunity cost" ... or more precisely, your "lost opportunities". This is what keeps career counselors and psychologists in business - the fact that people perpetually have to make decisions and make choices, perpetually giving things up and creating lost opportunities for themselves. There is fear and anxiety associated with the possibility you will make the "wrong" choice. And there is just as much reason to fear that you will fail to make any choice at all. Think of the deer, frozen in the headlights, failing to run this way or that way and ending up in the worst possible situation. Indecision and paralysis often go hand-in-hand. If you are going to move forward, you have to make a decision.

An engineer called me and asked me to help him make a decision on what to do with an offer he had just received. The offer was about 20% less than he was making at the high tech firm he was laid off from about six weeks earlier. The position is also at a much lower level than he was previously at. He told me that it was discouraging to receive the low offer but he was really interested in the technology the company uses and feels he can learn a lot. He also told me he was concerned that national and international economic uncertainty might make job offers scarce. And he was afraid of being unemployed for a much longer period if he didn't take the offer.

After exploring all of the parameters with him, I suggested that he take the job but that he also start working on a master's degree to

| RANKING | VARIABLES | R&S | CRO | SW | VT.CO |
|---------|-----------|-----|-----|----|----|
| 3 | LOCATION | 10 | 8 | / | 8 |
| 2 | PEOPLE | 10 | 8 | / | 8 |
| 1 | PROJECT | 10 | 10 | / | 6 |
| 4 | FUTURE PROJECTS | 7 | 7 | 7 | 8 |
| 5 | WELL RUN | 10 | 10 | 10 | / |
| 6 | PAY | 8 | 6 | 10 | / |
|  | TOTAL | 55 | 49 | 27 | 36 |

## COMPANY 1

## COMPANY 2

| PROS | # | CONS | # | PROS | # | CONS | # |
|------|---|------|---|------|---|------|---|
|  |  |  |  |  |  |  |  |
|  |  |  |  |  |  |  |  |
|  |  |  |  |  |  |  |  |
|  |  |  |  |  |  |  |  |
|  |  |  |  |  |  |  |  |
| TOTAL PROS: |  | TOTAL CONS: |  | TOTAL PROS: |  | TOTAL CONS: |  |
| TOTAL PROS - TOTAL CONS: |  |  |  | TOTAL PROS - TOTAL CONS: |  |  |  |

## COMPARISON OFFERS

Job Offer Ratings - 0 to 10

/ No data available
Instructions:
1. List companies that you have receive offers from
2. List the things that are most important to you when you consider an offer
3. Rank variables in order of importance to you
4. On a scale of 0 to 10 rate the variables for each company
5. Add up the numbers in each column to find the highest rated company
This candidate selected the second highest rated company because he had already worked one summer for the highest ranked company. The second highest ranked company matched the salary of the highest ranked company making it more competitive.

## PROS AND CONS TEMPLATE

Pros and Cons of Multiple Offers

List the pros and cons of each offer and then rate on a scale of 0 to 10

SEE MORE SAMPLE PROS + CONS LISTS
& DOWNLOAD TEMPLATES ONLINE
SERIOUSJOBSEEKER.COM

give him a safety net if he is still underemployed come two years from now. Two years from now, if the market is much better, he will graduate with a masters degree and will have great experience and be able to spring ahead. If he just takes the position and does not increase his level of education he is creating a benchmark for underemployment in the future and a distinct liability when he starts looking for another job in the future.

Another individual who was graduating with her bachelor degree called and told me that she has received an offer from one company but had several interviews yet to complete before she could make a decision. She would like to have all of the offers in hand before she made a decision, but she was getting pressure from the company that made her the offer. What should she do? How could she preserve the offer she already had without offending but still finish exploring all of her options?

The best way to hold off a company is to ask for enough time to finish your interviews and make a good decision. Most companies recognize that it is in their best interests if you make a thoughtful, unhurried decision. Some human resources people might try to pressure you to get an answer so they can move on to the next candidate if you pull out. If the company has to know right now, accept the offer. You can back out later with a "Dear John" letter. (Detailed in Chapter 7.1)

Usually, however, you won't have to

make a decision right there on the spot. If you can, you will want to take your time. When someone makes you an offer, be positive; let them know that you are interested. But tell them you need a bit of time to think about it, and to compare it with the other offers you've received. Anyone who is willing and able to pay you a salary is smart enough to know that if you make a bad decision, it is going to cost them. And if you take time to think and to weigh your decision, you are going to have more leverage when it comes time to negotiate the details. It's a lot easier to choose a good restaurant when your hunger is under control.

## 13.5

## EVALUATING AN OFFER

**Things to consider when evaluating an offer:** Have you done enough to know you have explored your options thoroughly?

• *Do you have enough information to make the decision?*
• *Do you like the work?*
• *Will you be learning something that fits with your interests?*
• *Will you gain valuable experience that you can use for your next move?*
• *Do you have a good chance to succeed?*
• *Will you be challenged?*
• *Could you thrive in the company?*
• *Does the work environment feel right?*
• *Do you like the people working there?*
• *Do you like your manager's style?*
• *How are the money and the benefits?*
• *Do you know what your other options are? Could you do better? Are you just taking this offer because*

*it is easy?*
• *Have you worked hard enough to get the right offer or are you being lazy and making due with less than you should?*

## 13.6

## THE FACTS

Finally there are some facts that you must understand when it comes to deciding on which job to take. You may not have done enough to get that right job.

Here are the facts:

FACT #1: *The average length of time it takes to get a job is three to six months.*

FACT #2: *Looking for work is a full time job. That means you need to work at finding a job 40 hours per week.*

FACT #3: *You need to commit yourself to finding a good job! The best use of your time is to find the best job for you.*

FACT #4: *If you waste your time on a substandard job, you waste your life.*

Just make sure that you are not selling yourself short by taking an inferior offer. You are worth more than that. You deserve a great job in a great organization where you can thrive and make a difference. Don't settle for anything less. Keep working until you find the right job in the right place. You will be glad you did!

# 14

# SURVIVING A LAYOFF

## 14.0

# THE VALUE OF POSITIVE THINKING

Being fired, laid off, or unexpectedly unemployed will test you like almost no other experience in life. It causes a terrible loss of identity. It can feel like you have lost your purpose in life. It causes depression for many people and it can create tension between you and your family and friends. It can be one of the loneliest and saddest experiences. A lot depends on your attitude, your coping mechanisms, and your support system.

The one thing you have to understand is that if you are reading this, you most likely do not qualify to be permanently unemployed. I say that all of the time to people I counsel through the job search process. It is true... I know. I spent 4 years with the California Employment Development Department at the beginning of my career and I know what permanently unemployed looks like. It is the person that no one wants to sit beside. It is the person who has zero skills, a seriously bad attitude, a really bad personality and probably smells really bad too. It is a package. My guess you do not have that complete combination of problems if you are this far into reading this so it is time to buck up! And figure out how to get out of this little blip on the screen.

I often speak with my husband Paul, a Clinical Psychologist, about stress and job loss. One of the major points he always makes is that it is not just a situation or an event that causes stress, it is how you perceive the event that really makes a difference. "One person might lose a job and be devastated; another person could see it as a challenge and an opportunity." Your

very success in life depends on being positive. A good attitude helps you deal with the stuff that comes at you in life. You are more likely to do well in life if you perceive the world as a basically friendly place, filled with opportunity.

I think it happens right when you are born. A nurse-fairy either sprinkles sugar, or squeezes lemon on your little noggin, and you turn out to be a happy person with a good attitude or you are an unpleasant whiner. And you wake up each and every morning with a smile on your face, or you wake up crying and screaming. That is how your earliest experiences are formed. Your parents either see that cute smiling face or they get jolted out of bed with your screaming, and they react accordingly. And all throughout your life people respond to that perception of you.

According to my husband, the psychologist, people either thrive and survive or fail in life based on their attitudes. "The most important attitude is referred as the "sense of coherence", which has three elements: a sense that you understand what is going on around you; a belief that you can handle things and take care of business; and a feeling that things are worthwhile and meaningful."

A positive attitude will lead to your success. Being positive is not only essential, it is also much more efficient. If you believe that you can handle things and take care of business you will set goals and map out a plan and proceed with it. Life is more manageable, and other people and opportunities are drawn to you. The converse is also true. If you are negative, you put out bad energy and no one wants to be around you. In life, there is not enough time to have a bad attitude. You will act based on your positive or negative view of the world. If you believe, for example, that there are no jobs out there, you will act accordingly and you will not be doing the things that are efficient like looking for a job.

## 14.1

Negative people also manage to thwart any opportunities that come their way. One close friend put it this way: "Being negative is a turn off."

Facing rejection is a part of interviewing, but you are not allowed to lose your positive attitude and your smile. And criticizing or complaining about a previous employer, or a project, or a team member, is the surest way to leave a bad impression. The result is that the employer is left with the sense that you have a problem or that you are the problem.

## ATTITUDE. EXERCISE. NETWORK.

*Attitude* - Hire a counselor or a coach if you need an attitude adjustment. It is important to know when to get help...

*Exercise daily and vigorously* - Depression takes a toll on your body. It will clear your head and help you move forward.

*Network* - Get out of the closet. You will not find a job in there... You need to get around other employed people.

So buck up! Recognize that you are a multi-talented individual who doesn't qualify to be permanently unemployed. You will get a job. You did learn a lot from prior jobs and from your training and education. Now figure out what the positive things are that you can share with the world, and get out there and work on it every day until you get to where you want to be. I love the quote from Thomas Jefferson: *"I find the harder I work, the more luck I have".*

Another quote that resonates with me: *"Whatever you think you can do or believe you can do, begin it. For in action there is magic, grace and power."* - Goethe

## KEEP CALM AND CARRY ON

During WWII, the British government placed inspirational posters in strategic spots all across England. London was being bombed relentlessly and people were on the verge of panic. The message was simple: *"Keep Calm and Carry On."*

Sometimes there is very little you can personally do to change things - you just have to keep calm and carry on. Recession is one of those globally devastating events that cannot be fixed by any one individual. No one escapes the reality of a bad economy. Recently laid off workers face tons of competition. New graduates are particularly hard hit by a downturn as they struggle to find their way in life. An entire generation of young people was caught up in the recession's paralyzing grip and will have to play catch up for a very long time to come.

Life until 2007 was soooo promising. Before 2007, technology, expected baby boomer retirements, and the constantly expanding global economy offered what appeared to be an extraordinarily bright future. For those who joined the ranks of the unemployed between 2008 and 2013, life was not so promising. It was, in fact, very challenging.

Keep Calm and Carry On. The message is two-fold. It is important to be calm, but you must also carry on. There may be nothing that you can do to end a recession, but there are things you can do to help yourself during trying times. Keeping calm and maintaining a positive attitude is essential. Carrying on is where the power lies.

Sometimes it is necessary to find alternative, legitimate uses of your time during a bad economic period. Carrying on means having purpose in your life even when you can not find some-one who values your services with a salary. You place value on your time by doing something of value.

I was reminded in a most graphic way about the consequences of doing nothing. I saw a young man who graduated in June of 2009 and had been interviewed for a very good job. A ton of other new graduates qualified for the job but he got the interview. As the interview progressed, the interviewer asked: "What have you been doing since you graduated?" It had been more than a year since the young man had been doing something really productive (being a student) and it was a legitimate question. The young man was perplexed by the question and answered, "I have been looking for work." The interviewer probed: "Is that all you have been doing?" The first answer was not impressive ... The real question the interviewer was asking was, "What have you been doing to improve yourself as you look for work?" The answer was: "Nothing." That young man did not get the job.

When times are challenging and you have to measure up. Employers will expect you to multi-task on the job so you must demonstrate the ability now. Besides looking for work, DO SOMETHING! Do something for yourself, do something for someone else...

You need to have an answer to the question, what have you been doing since you graduated or since you were laid off, other than just look-ing for work. Yes, looking for work can seem like an all consuming task, but it is not enough to impress an employer when you have been out of work for more than 6 months. Many people are taking up to two years to find work - and some people will become part of the per-manently unemployed as certain jobs disap-pear from the labor market forever.

There are a ton of people out there running a little faster and jumping a bit higher than

you are. People always say, "I don't have time to do anymore". When I was a student I took a class from the famous artist, Joseph Raffael, who said, "The more you do, the more you can do. The less you do the less you can do."

What do you need to do to make yourself an attractive candidate for your ideal job when opportunities are not quite so boundless? What will make you stand out from the pack? Take a career class, learn a new language, improve your computer skills, travel, build something, start a small business, volunteer at a homeless shelter ... the possibilities are limitless.

One construction management student start-ed his own home repair and remodeling busi-ness and even employed other students on the projects he took on. He had more work than he could handle while finishing his degree. Every job he did afforded him referrals to the friends of his customers. Every job he did was another reference for the incredible work he is capable of doing.

Sometimes it is a matter of being in the right place, doing the right thing, at the right time, organizing your luck by being ready for oppor-tunity when it occurs. Taking a career planning class or reading a career planning book goes a long way to preparing you to take advantage of the possibilities even before they hatch.

My all time favorite story is about a job seek-er in the last recession who could not find a position no matter how hard he tried. He had interviewed repeatedly with no resulting offer. He volunteered to teach a computer class at Mustard Seed, a school for homeless children. That so impressed the interviewers at a large state agency that they offered him a job.

One job seeker, who took my career plan-ning class met a hiring manager at a career fair during his last semester in college, and then noticed that the market was faltering. He wrote a letter offering to volunteer for the summer with the company he was most interested in.

The manager and the company president were so impressed with his approach that two weeks after he started volunteering they hired him.

Another job seeker who took my class met a manager at a career fair and requested an informational interview (on site company visit - a class requirement). During the visit he learned all about the company and they got a chance to look him over and see his enthusiasm. That (and having a resume ready) was all it took for them to offer him a summer internship that will last well into the fall ... this happened in the middle of the recession.

Still another job seeker who took my career planning class discovered that his current employer, Sacramento Regional Transit, would not be able to offer him a permanent position at graduation. He networked with the RT managers he had worked with. They put in a good word for him with a San Francisco consulting firm doing railway design and construction management. That connected him with a full-time career position that is just perfect given his interests.

Even in the tightest market, things are not always what they seem. If you only look at the bad news you miss the good news. There are always companies hiring. I read local and national stories about companies that are growing. For example, the Sacramento Business Journal is full of articles about companies that are expanding operations. A story I read a while back was about Altergy Systems. According to the Sacramento Business Journal, this company had 50 employees in Folsom and "plans to hire 20 more employees -- mostly in sales, engineering, and product line management -- by the end of the year". Now that's a tip!

There are things you can do now to enhance your chances. What are you doing with your time right now?

Keep calm and carry on.

## 14.2

# LEAVING GRACEFULLY: HOW TO HANDLE JOB TERMINATION AND START SETTING A COURSE FOR YOUR FUTURE

There are ups and downs in every career. My mom had a way of making even the worst crisis manageable: *"Into every life a little rain must fall..."* and *"This too shall pass..."* she would say. It had a way of putting things in perspective - life goes on.

If you get laid off, there are good ways of reacting and there are bad ways of reacting. Giving up and getting angry is not an option. Staying positive is the best approach. Often while people are being laid off, others are hired. Even in the worst economy companies hire, so do not despair and do not burn any bridges to your future.

As millions lost their jobs during the recession, there was no end of discussion about how to leave and how to survive. If you are ever faced with the unpleasant reality, you want to handle it in the most eloquent way possible. Your behavior is going to be judged and reviewed by your colleagues for years to come. Whether you know it or not, you are interviewing for your next job. People who move to other companies will decide if you warrant an invitation to join them at their new firm based not only on the work you did but on your tact and grace under "fire".

Being upset after a layoff is natural. It is one of the biggest rejections in life. It is like being served with divorce papers when you didn't even know there was a problem. You show up on time, do great work that is well recognized, and then *bam!*, out of nowhere, you get served with the pink slip.

To add insult to injury, while you are in the "layoff meeting" your are being locked out of your computer access and a company security officer is waiting outside your boss's door to escort you out of the building... oh yea, and your ID badge will be confiscated... It leaves you feeling like a criminal.

If you are the person who's on the way out the door with pink slip in hand and a box of your personal belongings, you really should think twice about telling everybody what you *really* think, especially in writing... Especially if you are angry, or hurt or resentful. *Do not do anything rash.* As you leave, do it like an Oscar award speech, thank everybody and their dog.

Consider this as a practical matter.

The people who remain behind are your professional contacts and may very well be the ones who help you find your next job. They may hear of a new job, or they may be planning their next move with you in mind. You do indeed want them to know how to contact you, but you don't want to leave any impressions that might cause them to hesitate before contacting you.

If you leave angry, you could be the one who reminds them that they hate their job just as much as you did. That increases the burden they carry as they continue. No reason you should remind them. And if they like their job, they are going to think there was something wrong with you.

You also want to make certain that you do not do anything that might cause anyone to question your judgment. Some of those you work with now might soon be in new jobs themselves. They might be starting their own business and looking to hire, or they might end up in a position where they can recruit or hire others in your field. The way you leave this job may be instrumental in whether you land the next one.

Keep in mind that losing a job is one of the worst experiences you will ever have in life. You are losing that daily contact with friends and venturing out into the unknown. You are bound to feel a sense of loss and disappointment. Indeed, it is not at all unexpected that you will experience a sense of depression. Writing on the topic: "Recession, Depression and Depression," my husband, psychologist Paul G. Mattiuzzi noted: "there is an extensive literature on the connection between unemployment and psychological well-being... work is often essential for psychological health."

*Networking your way to your next job starts the minute you decide what you want to do in life and continues until you retire.*

Always focus on the future. Start thinking about what next from the time you start a new job and definitely before all heck breaks loose. If the worst thing happens, my advice is that you leave graciously and effectively, with a seriousness of purpose. Positive is good, but it involves more than "just be positive."

First and foremost, make it a practice to have all of your contacts in an accessible database and that you always have an email address you can use for professional purposes. Gmail is great! Get linked on LinkedIn. Don't wait until you leave your job to start your professional network. Start this process from the moment you arrive in college and keep it going all through your professional life and into retirement. You are a professional! Act like one!

After a layoff, don't send anyone any email until you have collected yourself. That is always a good practice. *Never do or say anything in anger. It will come back to haunt you!*

Take time to exercise and reduce the shock and the stress of the "event". Fresh air will help you think about life and your larger purpose. Things happen for a reason. I rarely have someone tell me, after things sort out, that it was really the worst thing that ever happened. More often than not, positive things come from the challenge you face after a layoff. Change is good! Keep that in mind. *Also keep in mind that you do not qualify to be permanently unemployed.*

Once you have adjusted to the new reality, think about what you are going to say in your email to colleagues and friends. Let people know that you view this as an opportunity to explore your options, consider new directions, or to gain some education, training or experience that you have long considered. *You are the master of your future! Keep that in mind.*

If you have some enterprise or activity already lined up, let people know how you will be actively engaged and involved. Let them know if you have a side business or project that you will be focusing on (this is also an advertising opportunity).

If you know what your next career objective is, tell your professional contacts. Let them know what you are looking for. Give them your resume. Let them know that you would appreciate hearing from them, especially if they have any ideas or suggestions, or if they hear of any opportunities. Ask them to keep you informed if their contact information should change. Above all else, make certain that they know how to contact you by email, and through LinkedIn or some other location on the web where they can easily access your constantly updated resume and information.

The departure email is not where you want to share your feelings or look back on the past. It is OK to tell your colleagues and co-workers that it was a pleasure working with them, that you appreciate their support and/or friendship, and to express "best wishes." By way of your attitude, you want to let them know that you are not depressed and that you have passed The Serious Job Seeker IQ Test.

## 14.3

## WHAT HAVE YOU BEEN DOING DURING FOR THE LAST TWO YEARS? THE DODGE DURANGO ANSWER

If you have been out of work for a while, following graduation or in response to a downsizing, prospective employers are going to ask: what have you been doing during this time?

Dodge Durango nailed the answer in a 2011 commercial which you can probably still find on YouTube.

Here's the text:

*"It's 2011. Wonder where the Durango's been for the last 2 years? Well it toured around Europe getting handling and steering lessons on those sporty European roads. It went back to school - got an advanced degree in technology. Its been working out - more muscle, and less fat. It's only been 2 years but its done more in 2 years than most cars do in a lifetime."*

That's it. That's the entire message, the entire commercial is 62 words long but it gets the point across in magnificent form. The answer is straight out of Career Counseling 101!

Looking for work is a challenging experience. The more time passes, the harder the challenge. I have worked with people who have been laid off for up to two years. After being unemployed for a long time, it's a struggle to get back in the game. If you want to impress a new employer, one thing you have to do is to show them that you used your downtime time wisely and productively.

The recession is over, but the crushing reality is that many people will not break back into the market. Some people will be permanently unemployed or permanently underemployed. The longer the period of unemployment, the harder it is to break back in. The longer you are out and the older you get, the harder it is to get employers to look at you.

Even though we have just been through a terrible recession that saw even the most highly productive workers laid off, employers still wonder: what is wrong with you? why haven't you found a job? maybe your skills have gone stale … maybe you've lost your edge.

Companies are hiring again and employers are picky. The bar has been set high. You need to stand out and get attention in a crowded field. It's a basic supply demand situation: there are fewer jobs and there are tons of people chasing them.

If you are not productive during your time off, you are not going to be ready to compete. More importantly, you are not going to be able to impress anyone in a position to hire.

Phillip Tibbits, a career changer with 20+ years of experience, returned to school for his BS in 2007 and graduated in electrical power engineering in January of 2010. He started looking for work and after more than a year of looking received his dream offer from Puget Sound Power in Bellevue, Washington. During his long search for the perfect job, Phillip audited grad classes, joined the weekly alumni job club, attended professional events and job fairs, and put an extreme amount of effort into job seeking. He targeted specific companies, refined his search, and analyzed every interview to improve his performance. He also exercised daily and meditated frequently.

According to Phillip: "sitting in grad classes keeps you fresh and around people- it improves your mood. And students and professors are great sources for networking." Phillip said, "It's not just about looking for work, so you're breathing … what else are you doing?"

It is no longer good enough to just look for work or to just go to school. If you want to compete in the new, post-recession labor market, you have to do much more. You have to be able to demonstrate that you are constantly challenging yourself and exposing yourself to new life experiences.

When they ask about what you have been doing for the last two years, you need to be able to answer the way Dodge Durango did. Watch the commercial!

## 14.4

# PROTECTING YOURSELF AFTER A JOB LOSS

Unemployment is one of the most extreme challenges in life. It tests your character. It tests your mettle - your ability to face a demanding situation in a spirited and resilient way.

If you are laid off, getting a new job is a priority. But there are other things that require your immediate attention. The first thing you need to do is to apply for Unemployment Insurance (UI) through the Employment Development Department. The money is there to help sustain you at the minimum level while you seek other work. You are eligible if you have been laid off through no fault of your own from your last job, and if you are available for work and actively seeking work. File your UI claim as soon as possible after a layoff so that you can receive it immediately.

Second, you need to file for a COBRA on your health insurance or purchase health insurance on the open market. When you receive a jolt to the system like being laid off, your health can suffer and you can find your-self more accident-prone as you try to regain your sense of self. If at all possible, you do not want to be uncovered. If you are young you may be able to obtain health insurance through your parents or cheaply through the national health insurance program. I purchased Kaiser Health Insurance for my daughter during her job search, insurance that includes dental and vision coverage for a very reasonable price.

Third, you will want to reign in your spend-ing immediately. It is essential that you pre-serve your cash resources. Financial experts recommend that you have six months to one year's cash reserves to see you through a pro-longed stretch of unemployment. The average length of time that it takes to get a job is three to six months. Looking for work is a full time, forty hour a week job. Stop spending imme-diately and figure out how you are going to make it through this rough spot. If you are just starting your career, usher your resources. Ask your parents for help as you go through the job search. If you need to, get a roommate or live with your family to cut down on expenses. And do not make big expenditures that will burden you with debt. Even after you get a job, save for a rainy day.

After you attend to the basics, you need to concentrate on getting a job. Your attitude, beliefs and behavior are extremely important to your ability to get a new job rapidly. Don't stop looking for work because you think you need a break. Delaying a search just compli-cates things. Employers wonder what took you so long and worry you got a bit stale.

In the midst of the layoff trauma, it is im-portant to remember that you will get another job. I remember a VP of engineering who once told me that being laid off was an opportunity to reinvent himself. He had worked in a num-ber of start-up companies, as well as in larger engineering firms, and layoffs were a part of life. He explained to me that as an engineer, if a company has contracts and projects, then you have a job. If not, they cannot afford to keep everyone on through a downturn. He told me that he always found a better job, even in the tightest economy. Like I said... Attitude is everything...

# MANAGING YOUR CAREER

## 15.0

# MANAGING YOUR CAREER

Wouldn't it be nice if everything in life just fell into place? It would be so much easier if you could just relax and not think about your career. Imagine going to college, having a perfect job waiting for you, keeping on track for 40 or so years, and finally retiring in comfort. There are a few souls for whom this is possible. They were born into their destiny. For those of us who were not descended from royalty or didn't inherit the farm, it is a bit more difficult.

Chances are you were not born into wealth or you would not be reading this book. Most people have to work hard at figuring out their purpose in life, making things happen, and keeping things on track. Managing your career in this day and age is absolutely essential. Having a job doesn't absolve you from this obligation. Once you get the job you need to show up on time, have a good attitude, and do your best work. But that will only get you a paycheck.

If you are going somewhere in life, and want to have a little stability, you will have to take over the control panel and push the right buttons at the right time to keep your career and your life moving forward.

## RULES FOR MANAGING YOUR CAREER LIFE:

***Manage Your Manager*** - Start by finding the very best leader you can, and tie your string to that kite. If you find you are working for a dolt, find another boss. Work your way around the organization and see who is sharp and in-novative... aim to get into that group. If there are no smart managers to work for in the organization- find another place to work. You need to be challenged and you need to be happy. You won't be happy if you're not challenged.

The smart employer empowers you to do your job and encourages you to ever more amazing feats of brilliance. This ensures the success of the organization. The bad manager is just killing time (and the people under him) until he can impress his boss and get a promotion... not the best guy to work for.

***Never Stop Learning*** – It should go without saying but so often I see people who have stalled out... or attached themselves to a company that is locked in a time warp. Make sure your company is forward thinking and proactive in updating and changing with the times. Then make sure you are current and up to date, learning new things. Track down every training opportunity that is available to you - technical training, computer training, management training, communications training, customer relations training, conflict resolution training – go for it!

***Get a Graduate Degree*** - Good organizations not only encourage you to continue your education but they will also pay for your bachelor's and master's degrees with tuition reimbursement. You will have much more flexibility in a layoff situation if you are more highly educated than the next person.

***Get Licensed*** - If your profession has a licensure requirement or option associated with it- get the license, even if it is not necessary for the organization you currently work for. It is a no brainer and it is an insurance policy for the inevitable ups and downs of the economy. You will have more options if you get the license. You can always set up a home office in the backyard and go after business.

***Maintain a Contact List*** - Keep in touch with other professionals in your field who work for other companies.

They will be your life-line if you need to move quickly to another job. They will also be a good resource when you are stumped by a problem.

**Join Professional Organizations** - This is the absolute best way to keep up with what is happening in your field. You will receive journals and email newsletters that will keep you informed about all things professional - technological breakthroughs, emerging fields, political issues, licensing changes, and job listings.

You will also know when there are conferences and events that will put you in contact with other people in your field. This is soooo essential to your success. You need to be able to connect and network with people who are in other organizations that might provide you with upward career opportunities. Here is how it will happen: You will meet someone at a conference who has a new contract and there you go- an opportunity to move up!

**Take on Responsibility** – Smart companies in crisis look to keep the high performers. No one ever made a good impression by shirking responsibility. Stop hiding and volunteer for that big project. It will get you noticed!

**Maintain the Highest Ethical Standards** - Sounds like a no brainer but doing the right thing is not always easy. Sometimes it puts your job on the line to stand up and refuse to do something that is unethical. Personal values and professional ethics are all too often challenged in the work environment. You will know it when it happens. Walk away. You must trust the little voice in your head that your parents planted years or even decades ago. When 60 minutes, the State Licensing Board, the SEC or the FBI arrives you will be glad you weren't part of it.

**Anticipate Change and Be Prepared** – Most people can expect to change jobs about every three to five years and will most likely make a major career change three times in a lifetime.

Even the most charmed life has disruptions. You will discover that between technological, political, economic and social change – stuff happens.

**Be Aware of Changes Around You** - Read technical journals, business publications and a weekly news publication in addition to your usual news feed. Stay informed - big disruptive events rarely happen without warning.

Know what your next move will be both inside and outside of your organization. Stay informed about what is happening in your profession and in your industry. Keep abreast of the broader field you are in to identify areas of growth and companies that are innovating. Pay attention to world news - global events can wreak havoc on the economy - and your job.

**Maintain a Solid Financial Cushion** - When the economy is good it seems like it will last forever- it never does. Have a back up plan - a solid savings and investment plan goes a long way to helping you weather any storm that occurs. Have enough resources to last up to two years. It is as simple as spending less than you earn and paying off your debt immediately. Do both. You will sleep better at night if you know that you are covered even if you never use it. Lets face it - if you have ever been a starving student you have learned to live on less.

---

**Maintain a Career Binder
– Include in your binder:**

- *An ideas section.*
- *An accomplishments diary with pictures of projects and products you have worked on.*
- *A problems encountered, problems solved diary.*
- *An updated version of your resume and a cover letter template.*
- *A list of potential companies that you might consider allowing to employ you.*

All of these items put together will help you hit the ground running if the unthinkable happens-you lose your job.

Managing your career is not that hard. It just requires that you tend to it over time in a consistent way— just like watering the plants. You will be glad you did.

## 15.1

# QUITTING IS AN OPTION

Twice in one week, people came to me to ask if they should quit their jobs. I get this kind of question regularly. When faced with a really big decision it is hard to just do what you want to do. It is a dilemma. And it is paralyzing ... so many things ride on the decision.

A piece of you dies each day you spend in a job that you hate. To quit or not to quit, that is the question . "What should I do?" It is not an easy question to ask. We like to think we are in control of our own lives. Both individuals who came to me are at the end of their rope. Things had gotten so bad that unemployment seemed to be a better option than staying with their current job. Work got so unpleasant that it affected their health and happiness. A screaming boss was more than they could bear. Depression was a constant.

A career counselor's job is to help people sort their options and sometimes to give people permission to do what they want to do anyway. Sometimes the tough decisions in life are best made with a coach who helps you see all sides

of the issue. It could be a parent or a spouse, or a counselor who helps you decide. There might be something you missed in your analysis. But ultimately, you make the decision: stay or leave?

Here are the questions I ask:

- *How unhappy are you?*
- *How is your job affecting your life?*
- *Is your job affecting your health?*
- *How are you going to finance your search?*
- *Can you ask your parents for help?*
- *Have you done a budget with your current costs?*
- *What can you cut?*
- *How long can you last given available resources?*
- *How can you make sure you will qualify for Unemployment Insurance?*
- *What is your back up plan?*

Getting a new job is what people most want to accomplish. Up until recently, losing a job has meant that unemployment could stretch to 24 months. Having a back up plan means finding purpose in your life if you cannot find a job immediately.

The financial industry is notorious for MBS: management by screaming. One young woman who is the top producer in a financial firm, endured weekly phone "meetings" where her boss and her boss's boss ranted at her. The rest of the financial staff had been laid off, and for a long time she found herself waiting for the ax to fall. She survived all of the layoffs, but her quality of life suffered terribly.

In 2009, during the deepest part of the recession, I coached a VP of finance out of his position with a major bank. When he came to me he looked close to a heart attack. He had taken the job less than a year before and inherited a myriad of problem commercial real estate mortgages. He too endured a screamer boss. When he sought my help he was paralyzed. With the economy in free fall, he was afraid to quit, but he feared being fired. (Some companies use abuse as a tool to make people quit rather than having to fire them). He had a son in a private college and burdensome debt. He could not see a way out. The situation was killing him. He took the leap. He was highly motivated. I explained what steps he needed to take after leaving to preserve his ability to collect Unemployment Insurance to finance his search. Within six weeks of leaving his old job I coached him into a new job where his salary is much higher, and where he is highly valued. He is now in an industry that is not plagued by the mortgage mess.

A young engineer landed in my office just after being fired. His boss was relentless in his criticism and gave no instructions or encouragement. Constructive criticism would be nice.

Who knows why bosses scream. Maybe their job is in jeopardy and they figure this is the way to motivate the staff. Maybe they forgot that happy people perform better than people who are scared, nervous and unhappy…

Bad economic times bring out the beast in a lot of people. I have heard horror stories about screamer bosses who make life miserable for their workers. This is a vexing problem for many people because they feel they do not have the option to just quit - particularly in a recession. It is very hard to find another job when there is a 9+% unemployment.

In a good market, people have alternatives. They can just quit and find another job when things at work get too awful to endure. Quitting is it's own revenge.

Think of it like this: you are not stuck and helpless. You have options. You are not actually trapped by reality. You are only trapped by your fears. When you get rid of the fears, you can start to think creatively and discover the possibilities. You get to choose: is this a trap or

is it a challenge.

Maybe this is the time to jump. *Quitting is an option.*

## 15.2

# GOT BALANCE?

One of the most important things in life is to have balance. Having balance in one's life means that you are able to sustain yourself by working a reasonable number of hours doing work that you love, while having time to do the other things that bring joy to your life. Time for family, time for rest, time for enjoying friends, time for exercise, and time for vacations, in addition to working. Time to have a life… When work so dominates your life that you do not have time to enjoy it, you are in immediate as well as long-term jeopardy. Your stability, your health, and your relationships will be at risk. Some people don't realize it until it is too late.

I often speak to professionals who work 60 plus hours per week. It worries me greatly. The huge risk for a person with an unbalanced life is that it is unsustainable and eventually catches up with you. That is frequently why individuals seek my help in finding another position.

After coaching numerous people in and out of jobs, I have come to know first hand the ravages of working too many hours. A while back I was talking with a person who works in a high tech firm. He was standing outside of my office waiting for a graduate class to start. I said, "hi" and asked him what was new in his life and if he had gotten married yet. He said "no", and I said, "How old are you?" remembering him from one of my classes quite a few years back. He said 40, and that he hadn't had time to meet anyone because he works so many hours. I said, "Do you think this life goes on forever?"

I have also had occasion to work with people who have experienced serious repercussions from working too many hours under way too much stress. A while back I worked with two biologists who had jobs in high-powered firms, with tons of responsibility and very interesting work in genetics research. The problem for both young women is that they worked 60+ hours per week and were sitting, glued to computers moving around a mouse, for most of those hours. At very young ages, both ended up with severe repetitive motion injuries and were unable to work for a number of years. One was out of work for two years, and the other for four years. This is tragic. They are just now reclaiming their careers. And it is all too common.

In my classes, I have preached endlessly about working in satisfying, healthful environments, and about maintaining balance between work and leisure. Unfortunately, when people start jobs, they feel extreme pressure to perform and to deliver even on the most unreasonable demands. People are also pressured when there is instability. They feel they have to do more with less, and they feel uncomfortable requesting the resources they need to perform their jobs. They fail to request help, ergonomically correct chairs, or keyboards at an appropriate level for their height.

I believe that part of the problem is that people feel that they have no options. They feel that they must deliver or risk their jobs. But the more you do the more is demanded, or so they think. Trust me, if you are reading this, you are smart, you have options. There are times when you might believe you are trapped, but you need to get a grip on reality. If you are in a situation that is unbalanced, you need to assess your situation, explore your options and develop a plan for changing your situation. You only have control if you exert it.

I used to drive a little blue VW Bug. It was real cute. It had an air-cooled engine. What does that have to do with balance? Well, if the fan belt that turned the fan was too tight, it snapped. Just like in life. If you work too much, you snap.

## 15.3

# RESILIENCE

Resilience is a gift in life. It helps us recover quickly from the inevitable ups and downs that occur – a failed interview, the loss of a job, an illness, or worst of all - the loss of a family member. We all need to learn resilience to regain the happiness and joy in life after something bad happens.

Webster's defines resilience as the property of material that enables it to regain its original shape after being bent, stretched or compressed. So it is with humans. Everyone has disappointments in life. It is how we recover our shape and balance that really matters.

Resilient people manage to shake off the bad and recover their sense of self - fairly rapidly.

I encountered two job seekers who had experienced failure. Both were discouraged. After one bad interview, the first person wanted to just give up and take a menial job rather than pursuing a professional level job any further. He had done poorly in the interview and felt just awful. The other had had so many rejections he was in a serious depression – letting his appearance go and discontinuing any job seeking effort at all. In the process he was letting go his dreams of being an engineer after just three months of looking.

This is not good. Attitude affects behavior. When a person gives up on the future it is self-destructive. Accepting failure as a final destination is really not a good option.

NPR recently did a story on child educators who are focusing on the idea of resilience… teaching children "grit" - the ability to overcome failure or adversity and learn from it, rather than becoming discouraged.

I have often heard it said that we learn more from our failures than from our successes. I have also heard it said that things happen for a reason… It may not seem possible in the midst of a crisis but over time it becomes obvious.

People encounter adversity not because they are bad or careless, but because stuff happens that cannot be controlled. We cannot control what happens, but we can control how we react to it. If you think that a rejection or failure is the worst thing that ever happened, it will be.

If instead you think of it as an opportunity to improve or challenge yourself, it will be.

It is easier to get on with the next thing in life if you view bad happenings as something you can overcome.

Career growth, like a lot of things in life, requires resilience, agility, flexibility, and a positive attitude.

A friend of mine was rejected for a job a while back. He was disappointed but he didn't let it paralyze him. He grew in many ways – stepping back and working on things he was passionate about – building relationships, expanding a program, doing yoga, and developing a reputation for excellence. Now as he enters the last phase of his career, he has a position that is so much better and so much richer because he is so much better as a person and as a professional.

Time to regain your happy!

## ABOUT THE AUTHOR

**CICI MATTIUZZI** has worked in the career planning field for 30+ years.

Cici has coached and motivated thousands of job seekers and career professionals at all levels, from new grads just entering the labor market to executives moving up the ladder. In addition to coaching and counseling individuals, she regularly teaches career planning courses, workshops and seminars.

Ms. Mattiuzzi is a faculty member and the founding Director of Career Services in the College of Engineering and Computer Science at California State University, Sacramento (CSUS). She also worked as a counselor in the university Career Center and as an Employment Development Officer for the California Employment Development Department.

She has a Bachelors in psychology and a Masters in Social Science, with an emphasis on manpower and labor market economics.

For over a decade, job seekers have been empowered to achieve their career goals using books authored by Cici Mattiuzzi. In 2000, The Ultimate Career Planning Manual was published by the University bookstore, and in 2006, Kendall Hunt Publishing released The Ultimate Career Planning Manual for Engineers and Computer Scientists. In 2009 The Serious Job Seeker first appeared as an online job seeking resource and textbook and has received 250,000 page views from job seekers all over the world.

Ms. Mattiuzzi has authored and edited the weekly CareerUpdates newsletter (with a circulation of 6000 engineering and computer science students and professionals) for 20 years. Her articles have appeared in the press and in professional publications.

She has designed multiple software applications that have served to assist job seekers and to track employment trends. Ms. Mattiuzzi has supervised more than 40 teams of software engineers in developing, implementing and maintaining cutting edge career systems and services.

Ms. Mattiuzzi has organized and delivered the annual Career Day event for the CSUS College of Engineering and Computer Science for the past thirty years. She has hosted campus recruiting visits by hundreds of local, regional, and national employers, and has toured many of their offices, plants and facilities.

She consults with business, industry and government agencies on recruitment and talent acquisition, particularly in high demand and rapidly expanding fields.

*The Serious Job Seeker* is now available in print and kindle and *The Serious Job Seeker Organizing App* will be available in the Google Play store and iTunes Spring 2015!